ASPECTS OF
THE YORKSHIRE COAST

D1343364

Aspects *of the* Yorkshire Coast

Discovering Local History

Edited by
Alan Whitworth

Series Editor
Brian Elliott

Wharncliffe Publishing

First Published in 1999 by
Wharncliffe Publishing
an imprint of
Pen and Sword Books Limited,
47 Church Street, Barnsley,
South Yorkshire. S70 2AS

Copyright © Wharncliffe Publishing 1999

*For up-to-date information on other titles produced under the
Wharncliffe imprint, please telephone or write to:*

> **Wharncliffe Publishing**
> **FREEPOST**
> **47 Church Street**
> **Barnsley**
> **South Yorkshire S70 2BR**
> **Telephone (24 hours): 01226 - 734555**

ISBN: 1-871647-54-1

A CIP catalogue record of this book is available from the
British Library

Cover illustration: With thanks to North Yorkshire Libraries, Scarborough.

Printed in Great Britain by
Redwood Books, Trowbridge, Wiltshire

CONTENTS

INTRODUCTION

by Alan Whitworth

FROM LIFEBOATS TO WINDMILLS and from cinemas to the life of John Paul Jones, the American privateer, there is a purposeful variety of subjects in this, the first volume of, *Aspects of the Yorkshire Coast*. The success of the acclaimed Aspects series is based upon a simple but proven premise: local and family history is such a popular interest that a collection of well-researched and well-written articles by both experienced and new writers, relating to a single town and surrounding area or to an identifiable geographical district, will appeal to a wide readership. In this respect Wharncliffe Publishing have fully supported the project in an attractively presented and well-illustrated format which does not compromise on the quality of production whilst its editors always have an eye on academic standards.

The Aspects series was founded in 1993 with the publication of *Aspects of Barnsley*, edited by Brian Elliott, which was so successful that a further three annual volumes were published. *Aspects of Rotherham*, under Melvyn Jones's editorship, appeared in 1995, exceptional demand meriting a second volume a year later. Later, the series was extended to Doncaster, Sheffield, Leeds and now the Yorkshire coast with further new areas and subsequent volumes planned for Bradford, Huddersfield and Wakefield.

In this volume, aspects of the East Coasts' agrarian history are rightly given some prominence in an area where the influence of farming has played such an important role in shaping the local landscape. Windmills can be found in abundance in many districts, and are a feature that grew out of the grain belt which is so much a part of the coastal scenery from Whitby to the Humber peninsula. Edna Whelan's article on corn windmills demonstrates this fact in relation to one area, Scarborough and district, and shows the diversity and familiarity of these buildings.

Dovecotes, too, are an agricultural building considered in this volume. Little understood by many architectural historians and as a consequence, often overlooked, Reg Brunton describes and considers their role in the history of farming and their presence in the landscape.

The sea, of course, is a prime factor in shaping the pattern of industry on the East Coast. A dangerous occupation, many fishermen I am sure, would rightly praise the work of the Royal

National Lifeboat Institute (RNLI). In the story of the Whitby lifeboat, *Robert Whitworth,* we read of the dedication and heroism of these brave mariners as they set out in all weathers to protect and serve the fishing communities and sailors around our shores.

By contrast, a little hitherto aspect of maritime life is revealed in Dr Andrew White's article on ship carvings in the beautiful church of St Mary's, at Whitby, perched high on the cliff-top overlooking the harbour and fishing port, where for centuries sailors have worshipped while apparently surreptitiously cutting into the woodwork of the pews during services boat designs, and other graffiti, which has survived to this day, leaving a fascinating record of the life of our forefathers.

Tourism, today a major part of coastal life, is represented in the holiday journal of George Eaton, of Norwich, who came to visit this area in the nineteenth century and left behind a unique record into a months sojourn which he and his family enjoyed. One hundred years later, another aspect of tourism is recorded in the article by David Wright who writes on the cinemas of Bridlington, a form of entertainment which has kept many a holidaymaker content during inclement weather while staying at this lovely seaside resort.

Lastly, no Aspects volume is complete without some reference to family history or biography. Annie Parker's childhood memories will no doubt bring back similar recollections to many readers brought up in fishing communities, but her writings will also serve as a useful purpose for future generations.

Finally, this volume could not have been produced without help from a number of individuals and organisations. On the production side, Roni Wilkinson and Paul Wilkinson have made my job a lot easier and therefore deserve my sincere thanks. I would also like to thank all at Wharncliffe involved in the promotion support services for the book, including Chief Executive Charles Hewitt and in particular Imprint Manager Mike Parsons and Paula Brennan for sales and promotion; and I am also indebted to Brian Elliott for his invaluable assistance. In conclusion I should like to end this catalogue of thanks by expressing my appreciation to all the contributors who have written excellent articles that will hopefully inspire others to research aspects of the Yorkshire coast for the benefit of future generations.

Anyone interested in making a contribution to a future *Aspects of the Yorkshire Coast* should, in the first instance, contact the Editor, Alan Whitworth, c/o Wharncliffe Publishing, 47 Church Street, Barnsley. S70 2AS, enclosing a brief summary of the work.

1. HEARTS OF OAK – WHITBY WHALERS

by Kate Bonella

WHITBY, FROM 1752 TO 1837, WAS A WHALING PORT. Each full ship was estimated, by the Reverend George Young, to be worth about £3,000 to the town.[1] The most famous of the whalemen were the two William Scoresby's, father and son. During those eighty-five years, large numbers of men sailed from Whitby to the Arctic seas. They suffered hardship and danger and many lost their lives as they made their contribution to Whitby's wealth and prosperity.

Figure 1. A portrait of William Scoresby, junior.

The Penny Magazine for May 1833, published by the Society for the Diffusion of Useful Knowledge, contained an article on the whale fishing industry. Much of the information about whaling was taken from the book *An Account of the Arctic Regions* written by William Scoresby, junior (Figure 1), and published thirteen years previously.[2] It was then described as

> *a species of gambling adventure* [rather] *than as partaking of the nature of a regular brand of commercial enterprise.*

The description of the Arctic was of a 'desolate and inclement region' where the sea was 'crowded with new and strange horrors.' It was the sort of image that Mary Shelley had used in *Frankenstein*.[3]

Coal gas lighting and its effect on the whaling industry was the subject of an article in *The Times* on 30 June 1817. The argument put forward was that although it was cheaper than whale oil its use would eventually destroy 'one of our best trades and nursery for seamen.' These apprentices provided recruits for the navy from 'this most valuable and important' source. *The Hull Advertiser* for 15 September 1826, carried an article with a similar theme.

These articles demonstrate how important the navy was to Britain, and how important in the nineteenth century were the men within it, who learned their trade in the whaling industry. The skilled men and apprentices during the time of their indentures, had protection from the Navy's Press Gang. By contrast, the ordinary sailors were only safe from the beginning of February until the end of the whaling season. Whalemen were clearly regarded as an elite among mariners when they were needed.[4]

A single copy of *The Courier*, a newspaper published in London, is preserved in the library of the Whitby Literary and Philosophical Society.[5] This contains a report of a strike by the town's Greenland sailors. The men were demanding wages which 'considerably exceeded the wages given at Hull.' The strike was broken only when the boat *William and Ann* put to sea 'with such officers only as had agreed to the terms proposed' and intending to complete the crew in Orkney or Shetland. The sailors had not expected the owners to do this 'on account of an alleged scarcity of men at those places.' Within a few days the sailors had agreed to the owners' terms and conditions and the whaling fleet had sailed. The *Courier* praised the owners for resisting the combination of 'a few discontented but plausible dema-gogues' who had threatened a 'most valuable trade' in which all Whitby's artisans and tradesmen had an interest. There was no suggestion that the sailors might deserve a bigger share of the wealth produced by their work.[6]

The most detailed contemporary accounts of whaling are those by Whitby's own William Scoresby, junior, who later retired from whaling and took Holy Orders. He first went to sea with his father in 1799, aged about ten years. This may not have been unusual for captains' sons.[7]

Scoresby, like his father William (Figure 2), took the spiritual well-being of his crews seri-ously. His journal entry for the first Sunday of the first voyage of 1822 records that he had *Divine Service on board, morning and afternoon. . . In the evening we had. . . religious exercises with the apprentices, consisting of reading the Bible, singing and prayer: about fifteen of the officers and sailors also attended. I had a demand for all the Bibles (twelve in number) committed to my care by the Liverpool Marine Bible Society, for sale among my crew. . .*

Figure 2. Captain William Scoresby, senior.

It appears that he included religious instruction among the things its was his duty to teach to the apprentices under the terms of their indentures.

On most ships, according to Scoresby, other work was stopped but whale-fishing was regarded by the majority as 'a kind of necessity' because the whales might not be there the next day.[8] His Sabbath observances as a consequence, were not always popular with the crew. On Sunday 2 June 1822 he wrote:

> *Several whales were seen. . . and* Altora *was observed to have all her boats in chace* [sic]. *The harpooners were so tantalised by seeing whales in considerable numbers which they were not allowed to pursue that I was obliged to order them from the mast-head, and to run the ship out of the way.*[9]

The whaling crews also had a holiday from work on May Day. William Scoresby did not enjoy the festivities himself, but described how at midnight they began with the hanging of a garland of ribbons in the rigging. This was done by the man who had 'most recently entered into the state of wedlock.' Then a trio of sailors dressed as King Neptune and his wife and barber would board the ship. Greenhands[10] would be dragged before 'Neptune's Court' where the barber would lather their faces with a mixture of grease and soot and then shave them with a razor made from a cask hoop.

> *. . . a rude but active dance succeeded, sustained or directed by noisy vibrations of every kettle and pan. . . in the ship. . . The whole terminated with a loyal song which was chorused by the whole crew and then they dispersed with three huzzas* [cheers], *on a summons by the boatswain to 'splice the main-brace.*[11]

Scoresby did not describe the crews' accommodation apart from writing that he thought beds, in births or cabins, each for two or three men were better than hammocks, as part of his section on describing the ideal ship for whaling in volume two of *An Account of the Arctic Regions.*[12] In that book, and in his other work entitled *My Father,* he wrote about the treatment of a helmsman who fell into the sea in 1806, while Scoresby was mate on his father's ship, *Resolution.* After the frozen man had been revived, Captain Scoresby, senior, ordered that he should be put to bed between two mess-mates so that he would be warmed naturally.[13]

There are entries in a number of his journals (Figure 4) which relate to the provisioning of ship, about diet and there is also information about the sailors supplementing their diet with sea birds.

> *1813. 1 March. Whitby. Got on board twenty casks. . . of beer and*

eight casks. . . of ale. . . eighty bushels of potatoes, one ton of flour, thirty stone of oatmeal, together with sundry other stores.14

1818. 9 June. Finding our provisions rapidly on the decrease we took an estimate whereby we found that in seventy days fifty men had consumed 6820lb of beef and pork, 4700lb of bread, 1200lb of flour, 4000lb of oatmeal, a large quantity of pease and barley and about fifty bushels of potatoes. . .15

1810. 27 April. Lat 77o N Lon 2o E. A number of Fulmars having been caught, the seamen employed them in lieu of beef in the manufacture of lob-scause and sea-pies, which provided no bad mess.16

Fresh provisions certainly form the best preventives of the scurvy, and may be taken out in any quantity to the polar countries, without any preparation whatsoever; the action of the cold to which they soon become exposed, preventing putrefaction.17

He also wrote that crews were given extra 'grog' when they got wet or after work which had been particularly cold. As part of a description of crossing the ice on foot to pursue a whale which had dived below it, Scoresby penned:

. . .The shivering tars were, in general amply repaid for the

Figure 3. A representation of the ship *Esk* of Whitby, damaged by ice and almost full of water.

> *drenching they had suffered, by a dram of spirits, which they regularly received on such occasions. I have seen instances, indeed, of sailors having voluntary broken through the ice for the mere purpose of receiving the usual precious beverage.*[18]

Conditions of extreme cold were the subject of his entry for Monday, 29 April 1822. The temperature recorded fell from freezing point to minus two degrees fahrenheit. He did not mention here how the seamen or junior officers fared in their quarters, but did briefly touch on 'the extraordinary habiliments' that the sailors used as a defence against the cold;[19] however, another description of extreme cold does include a brief description of its effects on the crew members.

> *Some of the sailors suffered considerably from partial frostbite. The cooper had his nose frozen, and was obliged to submit to a severe friction with snow; and the boatswain almost lost his hearing.*[20]

The hours that the men had to work in these conditions varied according to what was being undertaken. On passages from one place to another the crew worked four hours then had eight hours rest. When they were fishing they alternated four hours work with four hours rest.[21] It is, however, apparent from descriptions that once a whale was sighted, frequently the whole crew was involved in its capture and toiled without rest until the task was completed.

Scoresby gave a very detailed description of catching and killing whales (Figure 5) and of the method of cutting up and storing the blubber. Three or four seamen, a harpooner, a boatsteerer and a linesman manned each of the small, open boats that were used to chase and catch the whales both in open water and among the broken ice. They were powered only by oars, the harpooner and linesman helping with the rowing when they were not 'fast'[22] to a whale.[23] The boatsteerer stood in the stern of the craft steering and encouraging the oarsmen with what Scoresby called 'encouraging exclamations'.[24] The harpooner was usually an officer, he struck the whale known as a 'fish', while standing in the bows. His harpoon was fastened to a line 1440 yards long. The lines were coiled in the bottom of the boat and were the responsibility of the linesman who saw that they did not tangle as the whale sped away.[25]

Senior officers spent hours up a mast, with very little protection from the elements, looking for whales. The crow's nest, which was invented in 1807 by Scoresby, senior, gave some shelter, but it was little more than a barrel with a moveable canvas screen to keep off the worst of the wind. On days when the temperature fell to below freezing it must have been very uncomfortable. As soon as the officer sighted a whale, from his perch high above the deck, he signalled to the watch below and a boat was lowered and rowed in he direction he indicated. A second boat was generally lowered to assist. As soon as the whale showed itself again the boats' crew rowed towards it as fast as possible. The whale would usually be on the surface for only two minutes and then would be underwater for five to fifteen minutes. During this time, according to Scoresby, a whale could travel as much as half a mile.[26] Part of the skill of successful whale catching was in predicting where

Figure 4. A page from Scoresby's 1806 Log Book of the *Resolution* showing the method of recording whale kills.

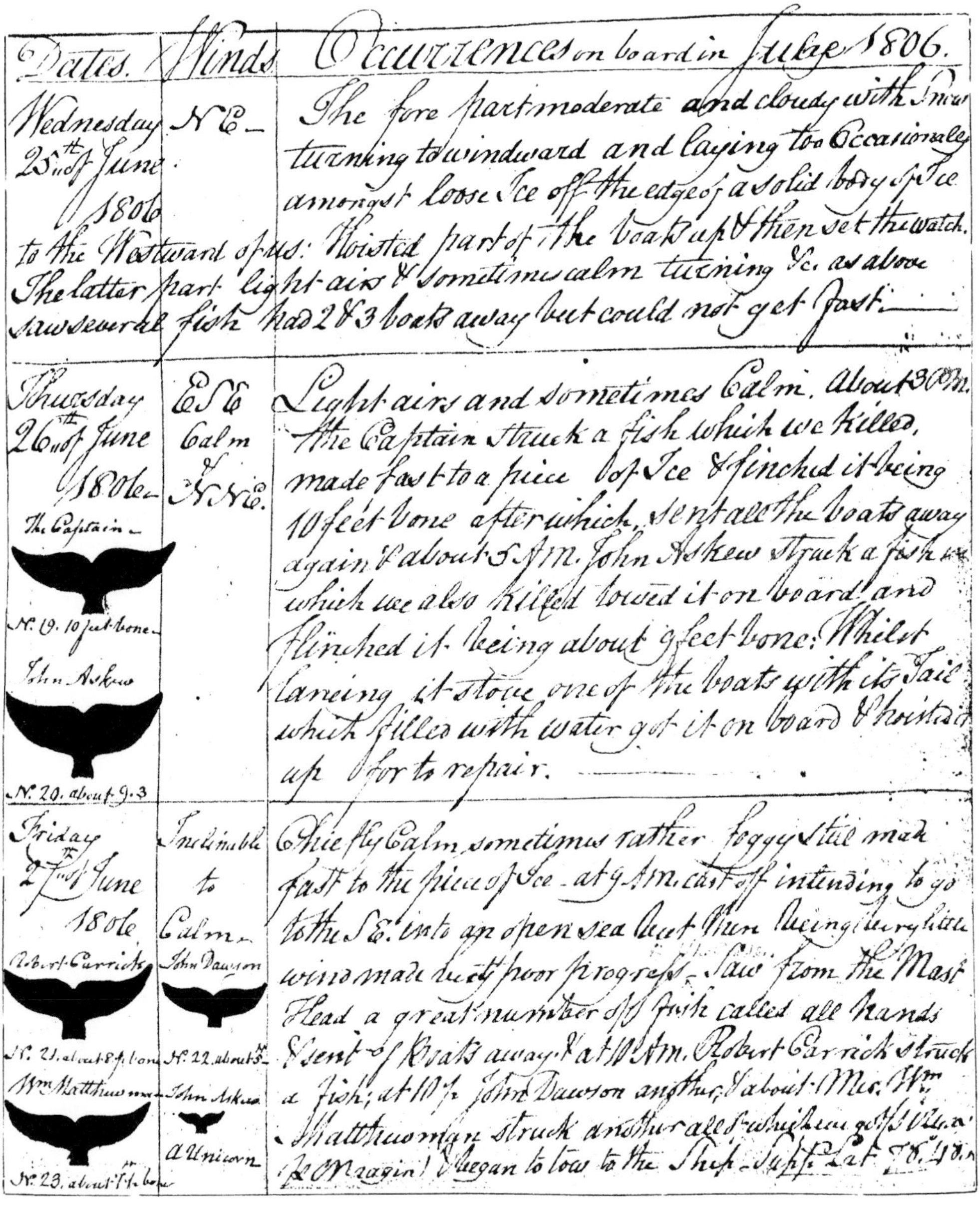

6 Dates.	Winds	Occurrences on board in June 1806.
Wednesday 25th of June 1806	N E —	The fore part moderate and cloudy with Snow turning to windward and laying too Occasionally amongst loose Ice off the edge of a solid body of Ice to the Westward of us: Hoisted part of the boats up & then set the Watch. The latter part light airs & sometimes calm turning &c. as above saw several fish had 2 & 3 boats away but could not get fast.
Thursday 26th of June 1806 The Captain — No. 19. 10 feet bone — John Askew No. 20. about 9.3	E S E Calm & N N E.	Light airs and sometimes Calm. About 3 P.M. the Captain struck a fish which we killed, made fast to a piece of Ice & flinched it being 10 feet bone after which sent all the boats away again & about 5 A.M. John Askew struck a fish which we also killed towed it on board and flinched it being about 9 feet bone: Whilst laneing it stove one of the boats with its Tail which filled with water got it on board & hoisted up for to repair.
Friday 27th of June 1806 Robert Carrick No. 21. about 8 ft bone Wm Matthewman No. 23. about 7 ft bone	Inclinable to Calm — John Dawson No. 22. about 5 — John Askew A Unicorn	Chiefly Calm sometimes rather foggy still made fast to the piece of Ice — at 9 A.M. cast off intending to go to the S.E. into an open sea but there being very little wind made very poor progress — Saw from the Mast Head a great number of fish called all hands & sent 5 Boats away & at 10 A.M. Robert Carrick struck a fish; at 10½ John Dawson another & about 11 Mr. Wm. Matthewman struck another also which we got [illegible] began to tow to the Ship — Suppd. Lat. 78.40 N.

the whale would surface next. If it was swimming close to the surface its position might be given away by the 'eddy' on the surface. Sometimes birds, which could see it from above and followed it for the scraps of food, would give it away. otherwise, the harpooners used guesswork, based on where it had surfaced previously, to predict where the whale would come up to breathe.[27] Sometimes the men would have to row for several hours before they caught up with the whale.

Ideally the men would approach the whale from behind, rowing smoothly and gently so as not to alert it and the harpooner would then be able to thrust the harpoon in just before the boat touched the whale. If they where not able to get so close, the harpoon could be hand-thrown eight or ten yards. When Scoresby wrote his Account, in 1820, a harpoon gun could increase the distance as much as thirty yards.[28]

The wounded whale, in the surprise and agony of the moment, [made] a convulsive effort to escape. Then [was] the moment of danger. The boat [was] subjected to the most violent blows from its head, or its fins, but particularly from its ponderous tail, which sometimes [swept] the air with such tremendous fury that boat and men [were] exposed to one common destruction.[29]

A man who could not swim had to depend on being able to catch hold of an oar to help him stay afloat until he was pulled out.[30]

The harpooner threw the line around a bollard in the stern of the boat, to slow the whale's descent since most dived rapidly when struck. The linesman often had to pour water over the line, as it went round the bollard, because the friction generated so much heat there was a risk of fire. His job in keeping the line running freely was vital as a fouled line could result in a boat being dragged under the water.[31]

The boat raised a flag when a whale was struck. A whale could run out the whole line in eight to ten minutes so the fast boat's crew needed assistance and more lines quickly. The flag was a signal to those on the ship and the men sleeping below were roused by shouts of 'a fall' and stamping on the deck.

. . .the crew would appear on deck, shielded only by their drawers, stockings and shirts, or the habiliments in which they [slept]. They generally contrive[d] to dress themselves, in part at least; as the boats [were] lowered down; but sometimes they. . . row[ed] away towards the 'fast boat', and [had] no opportunity of clothing themselves for a length of time afterwards.[32]

They killed the whale with lances, when it surfaced to breathe.[33] This was a bloody job and Scoresby noted that

The sea to a great extent around, [was] *dyed with blood, and the ice, boats, and men* [were] *sometimes drenched with the same.* [The whale's] *track* [was] *likewise marked by a broad pellicle of oil, which exude*[d] *from its wounds.*

It usually took about an hour to catch and kill a whale but the time varied from fifteen minutes to forty or fifty hours.[36] Boats could be lashed to the fast boat in an attempt to slow and tire the whale by increasing the weight it was dragging and so make it easier to get close enough to kill it.[36] In a long chase men would be rowing a small boat for hours in freezing conditions. At the same time the ship's captain or another senior officer would still be up the mast, directing the few crew members left aboard to keep the boats in sight. If the ship was able to get close enough, food could be thrown to them but this was not always possible in a ship dependent on wind and current for mobility and steerage.

Once the men had killed a whale, it had to be got back to the ship which might be some distance away. They cut two holes in the whale's tail so that it could be lashed to a boat. Holes were also cut in the fins so that they could be lashed together across its belly. Dead whales tended to lie on their sides or backs so that the harpoons stuck in the back were underwater. If the lines could be seen, they were hooked with a grapnel and cut, if not, two boats' crews held a line between them, dropped it under the whale and pulled it along to catch up all the lines which then could be cut free. The harpoons were left in the whale until it was with the ship and they could be conveniently removed but the crews had to haul cold, wet lines out of the water into the boats before returning.[37]

The crews roped their boats together in lines to share the work of towing the whale to the ship. Once there, the whale was fastened to the ship's side, then the dangerous, bloody work of flensing[38] had to be done.

...the harpooners, having their feet armed with spurs to prevent them from slipping descended onto the fish ...[39]

They were assisted by apprentices who were in two boats alongside with knives, saws and grapples.

Flensing in a swell [was] *a most difficult and dangerous undertaking ...The harpooners* [were] *...repeatedly drenched in water; and* [were] *likewise subject to be wounded by the breaking of ropes or hooks of tackles, and even by strokes from each others knives ...*[40]

Once the carcass was stripped it was cut free and sank. Scoresby could not resist the jingoistic comment :

Probably the average time with British fishers but little exceeds four hours; But I have observed a foreign ship [take] nearly twenty-four hours in flensing a whale.

The blubber was put in the hold until it was convenient to bring it up on deck and chop it up into pieces small enough to be pushed into casks through the bung hole. Scoresby found the nature of this aspect of whaling tedious but stated 'fifty men actively employed can prepare and pack about three tons of blubber in an hour.' He went on to say this is 'the most disagreeable business concerned with the fishery' because the blubber pieces had to be cut so small and because the decks became very greasy. Also the ship was unstable because of moving casks up out of the hold to fill them, lowest tier first.[41] However, curiously, he went on to claim that it was

. . .*not* [as disagreeable] *as generally supposed because of any disagreeable effluvia arising from the blubber, since the putrefaction of blubber is not at all offensive; and even after putrescence, we are not annoyed by it, there being nothing whatever unpleasant in the smell of a whale-ship, until after its arrival in port, where the cargo is unstowed.*[42]

William Scoresby, junior, recorded that whaling ships initially hired men who could perform the dual function of cook and surgeon. He believed that it was his father who began the practice of employing medical students or newly qualified doctors as ships' surgeons and gave them 'the advantage of a gentlemen's position.'[44]

One of these gentlemen was John Laing. He was employed as surgeon of the *Resolution* in 1806 and 1807. Laing published *An account of a Voyage to Spitzbergen*, in 1815. The section of the book that dealt with the whale-fishery was mainly based on his journal for the 1806 voyage. The *Resolution* sailed on 23 March that year 'amidst the hearty cheers of a numerous concourse of spectators' but struck bad weather and as a consequence Laing then suffered from sea-sickness all the way to Shetland 'from which the most experienced seamen were not exempted'.

Laing recorded that the *Resolution* carried nine months stores although the voyage was expected to last for only four or five months. The meat was not all salted as might be expected, since his journal entry for 3 May mentions that he ate fresh beef for dinner that

. . .*tasted as well . . .as if newly killed, as did the fowl we got at Shetland. These ere hung by the legs to a rope on the quarter deck . . Our eggs likewise preserved their good taste. This proves the antiseptic power of intense cold.*[46]

The Greenland men, as they were often known, probably ate better than many of their contemporaries on long voyages into warmer climates.[47]

In writing about his role as ships' surgeon, Laing said that he had encountered no scurvy, but found that coughs and colds were 'the most prevalent disorders. . . [while] fractures, dislocations, sprains, bruises, cuts and frost biting [gave] the surgeons a great deal of trouble' and added that 'a certain complaint' was very common.[49] Presumably this was a venereal disease which it would have been indelicate to mention by name in a book for general readership. Laing noted that the *Resolution* did not lose a single man during the two voyages; his recording of this suggests that the loss of life was not uncommon in the whale-fishing industry.

As surgeon, Laing's account of the treatment of a boatsteerer, who fell into the sea, is more detailed than either of the two accounts by Scoresby, junior.[50] When the man was brought into the cabin and undressed

> *His hair was like so many icicles and his body exhibited every cadaverous appearance. No pulsation was found in any part; and I held a mirror before his mouth without producing the least evidence of respiration.*

Laing then described the use of 'strong volatile spirits' on his temples, rubbing the man with coarse cloths and the application of hot flannels 'moistened with camphorated spirits of wine' to his back and chest. When none of this worked he had a sailor blow into the man's mouth until his chest rose. This early experiment with mouth-to-mouth resuscitation revived him. Captain Scoresby ordered the man to be put to bed, with a man either side of him 'to bring him the sooner to a natural heat.'[51]

At the end of the voyage Laing's journal revealed how seriously the threat of the press gang meeting the returning whaling ship was taken by the seamen who only had 'protections' for the whaling season .

> *July 27. Fourteen of our men being afraid of the Press, took two boats and ran into Robin Hood's Bay.*[52] *Anchored this evening in* [the] *Whitby Roads.*

The surgeon aboard the *Brunswick* of Hull, in 1824, was William Cass. He too, kept a journal. Early in its pages he mentioned 'family worship' in the cabin, twice each day, which continued throughout the voyage.[53] He also wrote about 'divine worship' on Sundays:

> *My reader may suppose it is a novel thing for sailors who have been for ages distinguished as such reprobates to worship their Master. . . it*

is with the greatest pleasure I record the alacrity with which the men obeyed the summons to attend divine worship which was announced by ringing the large bell.[54]

Later Cass recorded that

Captain [Blyth, Master of the Brunswick] *was furnished with some bibles and testaments which were all disposed of. . . a criterion if any was wanting of the reformation amongst the sailors*[55]

It was not only bibles and books the ship's master sold

. . .the masters of the whalers take with them coffee, sugar, tea, tobacco, stockings, mittens, flannel shirts and jackets. . . which are dispensed to the men when in need, assuredly was it not for such provision the greater part of the men would be destitute before the end of the voyage.[56]

This journal reveals that whaling was not all hard work. Cass recorded a 'whimsical and ridiculous custom' of the sailors as they rounded Cape Farewell on the way to the Davis Strait fishing grounds, that was very similar to the May Day celebrations, with Neptune, his wife and barber. In addition to being shaved the 'greenhands' had to had over a pound of tobacco or its equivalent in sugar or coffee to their mates.

Figure 5. Dangers of the whale fishery; a boat being attacked by a whale.

The ceremony ended with the men being served rum.[57] Another form of recreation was also described by surgeon Cass:

> *Sailors during the time they were beset in 1821 often amused themselves, when they were able to gain the top of. . . [ice]bergs, by sliding down the mountains, on a piece of board, into the valleys below.*[58]

For William Cass, the Arctic was a beautiful and awe inspiring region. He wrote :

> *In the evening the atmosphere was clear, when the sky was beautifully and brilliantly illuminated by that remarkable aerial phenomenon denominated Aurora Borealis or Northern Lights.*[59]

In a passage much more emotional than many other writers' scientific observations, he described something that had affected him deeply :

> *It is probable that the most terrific and sublime spectacle in nature is the concussion of these enormous fields and floes [of ice]. It would be difficult for the human imagination to conceive anything more awful and impressive than the sensation produced on the minds of the crew of a solitary ship working her way through the regions of eternal frost under a dark and lurid atmosphere and the sun obscured by dense vapours, when the still and utter silence which had reigned around is suddenly and fearfully interrupted by the meeting of two enormous fields or floes. . . the one is broken and destroyed or forced in part above the other with loud and terrible dissonance resembling the voice of thunder or the roaring of canon.*[60]

This kind of reaction to the Arctic could have been a powerful inducement to any sailor to return to these regions every year with the whaling fleet.

Thomas Gowland was the mate of the ship *Neptune,* of Hull, in 1820. His journal mentions only two captains by name.[61]

> *May 5th. . . Spoke* [to] *Captain Scoresby of the* Baffin, *of Liverpool - no whales.*
> *May 30th. . . Spoke to the* Fame, *Captain Scoresby, senior, with six whales, 24 tons of oil.*

Clearly the two Scoresby's were well-known amongst their peers and Gowland wanted to record his contact with them. Whitby's present pride in its heroes echoes this too.

The daily record of Gowland's ship notes that on 31 March, four of the crew were in Lerwick goal. They were brought before the magistrates the following day when one turned King's Evidence and informed on his mates as a result of which, the other three were fined twenty-two shillings each. On 2 April all the crew went ashore to attend church. Gowland did not record whether this act of contrition had any connection with whatever incident had put the four crewmen in prison.

There are a few tantalising personal glimpses of the crew's lives in Gowland's journal:

> *May 26th. . . From repeated inattention and negligence of duty Thomas Pinkney was displaced from the situation of boatsteerer to that of line manager.*
>
> *August 6th. . . [Lerwick] Thomas Pinkney went on shore without leave and not only neglected his duty whilst there but returned in a state of intoxication and behaved on board in a most mutinous manner.*

Pinkney's fate was not recorded and we can only speculate as to whether his 'repeated inattention and negligence' were symptoms of an alcohol-related problem brought about by the hard regime of life on board a whaling vessel.

Two working-class autobiographies contain accounts of a season's whaling. A brief account of a voyage from an ordinary sailor's point of view is given in the life story of John Nichol. He was a mariner who dictated his autobiography when aged sixty-two years old, in 1822. Nichol was cooper aboard the ship *Leviathan*, of London, in the year 1784. During its voyage the ship was beset by storm for ten days and he did not enjoy the experience as his tale recalls.

> *As far as the eye could see all was ice, and the ship so pressed by it, everyone thought we must either be crushed to pieces, or forced out upon the top of the ice, there ever to remain. At length. . . the weather moderated. . . it was a reprieve from death. The horrors of our situation were far worse than any storm I was ever in. . . Locked up in ice all exertion is useless, . . you must behold, in all its horrors, your approaching fate, . . while the cracking of the ice, and the less loud but more alarming cracking of the vessel, served to increase the horrors of this dreadful sea-mare.*[62]

Earlier comments by Nichol show that he was not particularly afraid of storms at sea. The feeling of helplessness that was caused, for him, by the inactivity of being hemmed in by menacing ice was something that he did not wish to repeat (Figure 3). John Nichol remembered no beauty in the Arctic and did not wish to return.

> *I did not like the whale fishery. . . Desolation reigns around; nothing but snow, or bare rock and ice. . . I felt so cheerless that I resolved to bid adieu to the coast of Greenland for ever. . .*[63]

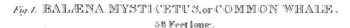

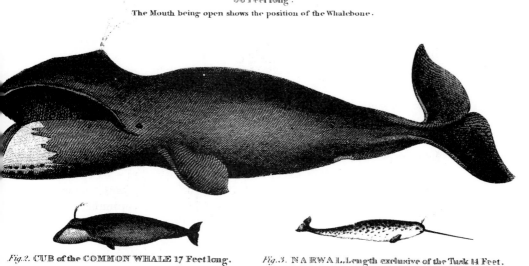

Figure 6. An enraving of the *Balaena Mysticetus*, or Common Whale.

Nichol told how the ship returned full with only four whales (Figure 7) so he had not had many experiences of a successful chase. However, thirty-eight years after he served for that single season of whaling his most vivid impression of the Arctic that he retained and wanted to communicate was one of desolation and fear.

Another seaman's autobiography containing an account of a single season's whaling, is that of Christopher Thomson, written when he

Figure 7. The whaling ships *Phoenix* and *Camden* entering Whitby harbour from Greenland. *From the book* The Wooden Ships of Whitby *by J R Bagshawe*

was aged around forty-seven years. he had been apprenticed as a ship-builder but, aged twenty 'as shipbuilding was now at a low ebb, [he] secured a chance to serve as a carpenter's mate to Greenland.'[64] This was in 1820, the year in Scoresby published his *Account*, but Thomson's description of his fellow sailors, aboard the *Duncombe*, of Hull, is quite different from that of Scoresby. He wrote that the Greenland sailors were not only 'notorious for their daring' but also for their 'disrespect of speech'.

> *Even in those days of uncouth language, a 'Greenlander's galley' was proverbially the lowest[65] . . .in 1820 it might be said, that in a Greenland-man's galley, licentiousness sat enthroned.*[66]

Only two or three of the crew of the *Duncombe* had bibles but Thomson claimed that they were exceptions 'being Dissenters - I believe Methodists'. These few were 'the butt of our boasted tars'.[67] That Thomson mentions this, however, does not necessarily contradict the evidence of Scoresby, Laing and Cass on the subject of religious obser-vances aboard other ships. Regular sailors would have known the captains by repute, and so could have chosen whether or not they sailed with those who held divine service and carried bibles.

As a carpenter, Thomson was 'admitted to the half-deck' with the harpooners and officers, whilst ordinary sailors, boatsteerers and linesmen were restricted to the galley, 'and frequent were the petty jealousies, gibes and sarcasms engendered by this division of parties'.

Thomson appears to have felt himself intellectually superior to the rest of the half-deck crew, evident in his recording that

> *Their leisure hours were frittered away in low conversations, . . .card playing and a song were their higher qualifications. A book was a rare thing among them; . . .*

The whole ships company received their 'mess-pots, or drams' every Saturday night, but many of the crew saved their ration so that they could 'treat . . .any friend who might board during the voyage'.[68] This indicates that visits of crew between ships was common when they were close to each other.

He wrote about the rush for the boats when a whale was struck. To be amongst the last boat crew to be lowered was considered contemptible. To be the last man to the boats two or three consecu-tive times was 'quite enough to stamp the fellow a lubber'.[69]

Thomson was aware that many of the crew found an excitement in whaling that he did not share but, clearly, he felt that the ordinary sailor was being exploited. He described the thrill of the whale hunt very sarcastically. The following description of dragging a boat over the ice in chase of a whale is typical.

> *They have to drag for miles over the surly field. Are they tired? What if they are? They must not even think of it, much more complain - for to name it would rank mutiny against the blubber lords! So tug on, brave hearts! Plash, plash through knee-deep lakes of half thawed ice; it freezes keenly, and soon your trousers will make shields of icicles. 'We shall kill her yet, and then my brave fellows, if she measures well, you shall have twenty shillings and a mess-pot of rum, if she is not full-size-bone, you must hope for better luck next time; and be content to know, that whether she measures or not, the merchant will get his scores of pounds - tug on brave hearts, we shall kill her yet!*[70]

After six hours on the shifting ice they were no nearer the ice-lake they were trying to reach. 'A poor Shetlander' lay down to sleep and by the time his mess-mates missed him and hurried to wake him he had died.[71] Thomson had a good reason for his anger towards the 'blubber lords'.

In detail he recounted the most bloody aspect of the job. After killing a whale the men were 'drenched' with the whale's blood and the sea 'stained with her gore'.[72] The flensing was so dirty he said, that

> . . .*the sailors put on an old dress, usually so patched, that it would have been difficult to find a 'ragman' in the home market that would [have] speculate threepence on it. This dress [was] mostly thrown overboard when the season [was] over.*[73]

He also detailed the sailors clothing for cold weather.

> . . .*two or three shirts, flannel and striped cotton, two pairs of stockings, worsted or flannel draws, two pairs of trousers, two waistcoats, an underjacket and pea-jacket, two or three pairs of*

Figure 8. A diagram of an oil refinery in which the whale blubber was rendered into oil. *From a drawing by Roger Finch*

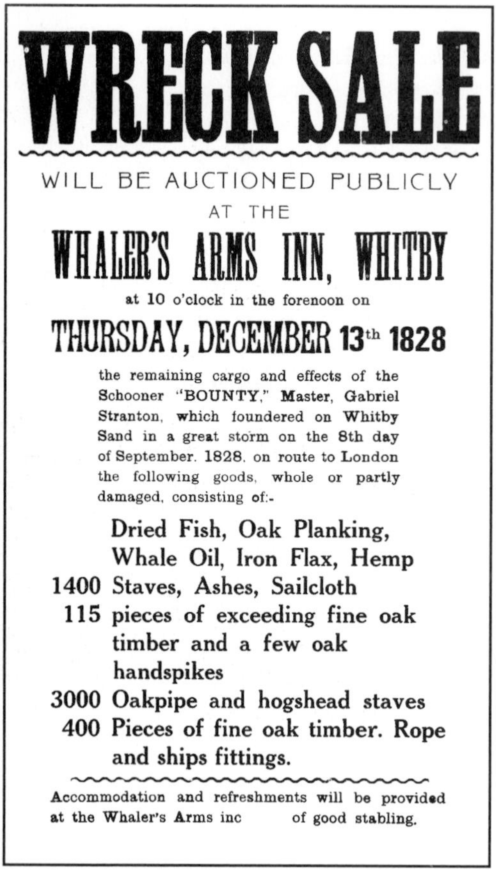

WRECK SALE

WILL BE AUCTIONED PUBLICLY
AT THE

WHALER'S ARMS INN, WHITBY

at 10 o'clock in the forenoon on

THURSDAY, DECEMBER 13th 1828

the remaining cargo and effects of the Schooner "BOUNTY," Master, Gabriel Stranton, which foundered on Whitby Sand in a great storm on the 8th day of September. 1828. on route to London the following goods, whole or partly damaged, consisting of:-

Dried Fish, Oak Planking, Whale Oil, Iron Flax, Hemp

1400 Staves, Ashes, Sailcloth

 115 pieces of exceeding fine oak timber and a few oak handspikes

3000 Oakpipe and hogshead staves

 400 Pieces of fine oak timber. Rope and ships fittings.

Accommodation and refreshments will be provided at the Whaler's Arms inc   of good stabling.

Figure 9. A poster announcing the sale of goods of the schooner Bounty, 1828, to be held at the *Whalers Arms Inn.*

mittens, and a wig of lambs-wool, which fits so closely around his head that little more than the face is exposed, and the tar peeps through his bale of clothing like an owl from the scooped orifice in a five century grown oak. [74]

For Christopher Thomson, one season of whaling was enough.

Scoresby's description of the work of whale fishing shows that all members of the crew were involved. Different jobs required different abilities and skills, but they were all important and dependent on each other for both their safety and their success. The ability of the oarsman to continue rowing for long periods while muffled in their 'extraordinary habiliments' was as important as the accuracy of the harpooner or the ability of the captain to direct the ship safely through the ice. Officers were fully involved in catching whales too, doing the jobs that required the most skill.

In their writings about the whaling industry, Scoresby, Laing and Cass seem to have been most concerned to show the whaling crews in a good light. They emphasised both their bravery and their Sabbath observance. This emphasis suggests that whalers may have had a poor reputation among the sailing fraternity which they wanted to improve. The picture that emerges from Scoreby's writing is one of periods of hard work and danger for the sailors interspersed with periods of calm when there were no whales near

For those who were satisfied with their share of the profit or hoped for promotion, the Arctic could be a place of excitement and opportunity. Even Thomson could not entirely resist the thrill of the hunt. The beauty that Nichol could not see was a major part of the Arctic's attraction to many others. Whalers formed a small community held together by common danger and loyalty, their safety depended on everyone from captain to cook doing their job well. This sense of community may have been another form of attraction for some of the seamen who went out whale hunting.

Notes and References

1. Young, Reverend George *A History of Whitby and Streonshalgh*, Whitby, 1817, Vol.2 p.566
2. Scoresby, William *An Account of the Arctic Regions with a History and Description of the Northern Whale-fishery*, Edinburgh, 1820; hereafter referred to as Account
3. Shelley, Mary *Frankenstein*, London 1818.
4. The accounts of *Henrietta*, of Whitby, include 'Lads protection 5/-' for 1777-8 and in 1794 'To Jarrat applying to the Admiralty to get a sailor cleared from man of war £3 3s 0d'
5. *The Courier*, 31 March 1818
6. Average earnings from a voyage, producing a good cargo of 200 tons of oil, were given by Scoresby in 1820, as : Master from £250 - £600 depending on oil prices; Chief Mate £95; Common Sailor £25.
7. An unpublished account of a mariner's exploits *Memorandum of the Life of J.C.* records that Joseph Christie, born 1773, sailed on the *Ulysses* with is father, in 1784, from London to the Greenland seas.
8. Scoresby, William *Memorials of the Sea Sabbaths in the Arctic Regions,* London, 1851, pp.8-9.
9. Scoresby, William *Journal of a Voyage to the Northern Whale-fishery including Researches and Discoveries on the Eastern Coast of West Greenland made in the Summer of 1822 in the Ship Baffin of Liverpool;* hereafter referred to as Journal.
10. 'Greenhands' were those men who were on their first voyage in the Arctic.
11. Scoresby *Journal* pp.34-8.
12. Scoresby *Account* Vol.2 pp.181.
13. Scoresby *Account* Vol.2 pp.360-1; Scoresby, William, junior My Father, London 1851 pp.127-9.
14. Quoted in Stamp, Tom and Cordelia *Greenland Voyager.* Caedmon, Whitby 1983, p.33.
15. quoted in *ibid* p.33.
16. quoted in *ibid* p.36.
17. Scoresby *Account* Vol.1 p.30 footnote.
18. *ibid* Vol.2 p.272.
19. Scoresby *Journal* p.31.
20. *ibid* p.44.
21. Scoresby *Account* Vol.2 p.235.
22. A 'fast' boat was one that had harpooned a whale. A 'fast' whale was one that had been harpooned.
23. Scoresby *Account* Vol.2 p.235.
24. *ibid* Vol.2 p.235.
25. *ibid* Vol.2 p.232.
26. *ibid* Vol.2 p.245.
27. *ibid* Vol.2 p.240.
28. *ibid* Vol.2 p.242.
29. *ibid*.
30. *ibid* Vol.2 p.246.
31. *ibid* Vol.2 p.245.
32. *ibid* Vol.2 p.242. This description of what the men wore in bed suggests that their accommoda-

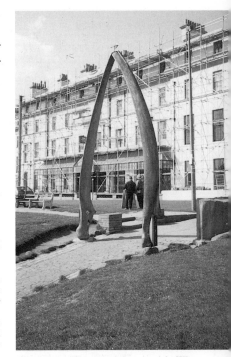

Figure 10 The whalebone arch, West Cliff, set up to commemorate the whaling industry in Whitby.
Photograph by Alan Whitworth

tion was reasonably warm.

33. *ibid* Vol.2 p.248.

34. *ibid.*

35. *ibid* Vol.2 pp.250-1.

36. *ibid* Vol.2 p.284.

37. *ibid* Vol.2 pp.293-4.

38. Flensing is the work of stripping the blubber from the whale carcass. The blubber is a layer between the outer skin and the inner flesh.

39. *ibid* Vol.2 pp.298-9.

40. *ibid* Vol.2 p.299.

41. *ibid* Vol.2 p.304; Scoresby Journal p.48.

42. Scoresby *Journal* pp.48-9.

43. Scoresby *Account* Vol.2 p.311.

44. Scoresby *My Father* p.71.

45. Laing, John, Surgeon *An Account of a Voyage to Spitzbergen containing a full Description of that Country, the Zoology of the North and of the Shetland Isles with an Account of the Whale-fishery.* Mawman & Brown, 1815, p.7.

46. *ibid* p.69.

47. A weekly list of provisions for one man aboard the ship Gilmore in the late 1830s records Sunday 24oz beef and 1pt flour; Monday 24oz pork and half pint of peas; Tuesday 24oz beef and 16oz potatoes or half pint of rice or 1 pint flour; Wednesday as Monday; Thursday as Sunday; riday as Monday; Saturday as Tuesday; plus 12oz sugar per week; ounce and a half of tea per day; one and half pints of vinegar per week; 6oz of bread per week. Howard, John *Master Mariner Extraordinary; The Life and Times of Captain Edward Theaker of Staithes 1786-1865.* Regional Studies Series 1 No.2, 1995, p.112.

48. Laing *Account* p.41.

49. *ibid* p.157.

50. Scoresby *Account* Vol.2 p.360; *My Father* p.127-9.

51. Laing *Account* pp.149-51.

52. Robin Hoods Bay is on the coast about five miles south east of Whitby.

53. Credland, Arthur G (editor) *The Journal of Surgeon Cass Aboard the Whaler 'Brunswick' of Hull 1824.* Humberside Libraries and Arts, 1988, p.21. The phrase 'throughout the voyage' suggests that this journal was revised or added to after the actual voyage itself.

54. *ibid* p.28.

55. *ibid* p.27.

56. *ibid.*

57. *ibid* p.32.

58. *ibid* p.37.

59. *ibid* p.30.

60. *ibid* p.35.

61. Gowland, Thomas *Log of a Voyage from Hull towards Greenland in the Ship Neptune, Martin Monroe Commander, 1820.* National Maritime Museum, Lubbock Collection.

62. Grant, Gordon *The Life and Adventures of John Nichol Mariner,* Cassell & Co, 1937, p.73.

63. *ibid* p.74.

64. Thomson, Christopher *The Autobiography of an Artisan,* London 1847, p.117.

65. *ibid* p.118.

66. *ibid* p.128.

67. *ibid* p.121.

68. *ibid* p.128.

69. *ibid* p.139.

70. *ibid* p.144.

71. *ibid* pp.144-5.

72. *ibid* p.145.

73. *ibid* p.150.

74. *ibid* p.149.

2. John Paul Jones – The Turncoat Hero

by Jack Storer

JOHN PAUL JONES, THE NOTORIOUS PRIVATEER, was once the scourge of the East Coast in and about the year 1779. Although a Scot by birth, he held for a period a commission in the American Navy at the time of the War of Independence, and played havoc with the local shipping during that conflict. Yet while an enemy of the English, he was nevertheless held in high regard, especially after his most notable escapade, the capture of the British warship, HMS *Serapis* against tremendous odds following the battle of Flamborough Head on 23 September 1779, described as 'the most remarkable naval victory on record.'

Born in 1747 at Kirkbean, Galloway in south-west Scotland, his father John Paul, was a gardener on the Abigland estate. While no doubt many thought he should be content to follow his father on to the land, John Paul, junior, had other ideas, and from a very early age, he was transfixed by the ships plying their way along the Solway Firth between Dumfries, Whitehaven, Liverpool and the Americas, where an elder brother had settled in Virginia as a tailor.

Christened plain John Paul, he grew up without money or connection in an age when both were necessary for advancement; but he had a deep love for Scotland, for the romantic tales of Scottish resistance to British rule and, above all, for the possibilities of adventure and fame that the sea inspired - so at the tender age of thirteen, he enlisted in the merchant service as an apprentice to a ship-owner in Whitehaven, Cumbria, 36 miles south-west of Carlisle, determined to make his fortune and improve his social station in life.

In his first year at sea, he sailed first to the West Indies, then to Virginia on the brig *Friendship,* and over the following years he made several voyages to the New World, which he came to know and admire; and once, entirely against his will, he was forced to serve on slave ships - 'black-birders' - whose brutal and miserable conditions he abhorred. As soon as feasible he quit this 'abominable trade' in exchange for service on merchant vessels, armed or otherwise, slowly improving his navigation and working his way up the ranks. In 1768, he proved his worth when, on the return voyage from the West Indies, both the master and mate of the small brig *John* died of fever and, aged only twenty-one, he brought the ship safely back to Scotland. The following year he made his maiden voyage to Jamaica as the appointed captain of the *Betsy*, and with subsequent voyages to the West Indies and the captaincy both his career and character matured, and Captain John Paul looked set to achieve his goal of a comfortable and respected life.

In 1774, however, at the age of twenty-five, John Paul could not have envisaged what fate had in store. As captain of the merchant ship *Betsy*, he had entered into a profitable partnership with a merchant-planter of Tobago, and over the years he had amassed a considerable fortune of £2,500. At last, the prospect of retiring to become a gentleman planter in Virginia, which he had first visited in 1761, seemed a real possibility Unfortunately, in one terrible incident, all this was dashed from his grasp, when a virulent clash broke out between captain and crew while the *Betsy* was docked in Tobago, and John Paul was forced to defend himself against a mutineer sailor who he killed in the ensuing conflict. As the sailor was a popular native character from that place, it was suggested that if he gave himself up to the authorities he would be unlikely to receive a fair trial - so he fled the *Betsy* to America and changed his name.

Adding Jones to his name after the Jones family with whom his brother William was living, John Paul Jones settled down near his sibling in Fredericksburg, Virginia, and paid keen attention to the first stirrings of the War of Independence. It was at this time when fighting broke out between England and the Thirteen Colonies that the American Navy was set up, known by the name of the Continental Navy.

The first Continental Navy, consisting of two armed merchant ships, two armed brigantines, or brigs, and one armed sloop, was created by Act of the Second Continental Congress on 13 October 1775. Maryland's delegate to the Congress, Samuel Chase, summed up the general scepticism this undertaking provoked when he called it, 'the maddest idea in the world'. The most thorough-going critics, who generally came from non-mercantile areas inland of the American coast, questioned whether there was any point in the colonies going to great expense to become a sea power. The vast body of opinion though, did not doubt that America desperately needed a navy.

By comparison, the British - or Royal - Navy at this date, truly did rule the waves. In the 1770s, the Britannic fleet comprised of one hundred ships of the line - that is, warships with over sixty guns. The Netherlands had only eleven ships of the line. The colonies had none. Their largest warship, the 350 ton *Alfred*, had only thirty guns, and, quite apart from the number of guns, the American navy had only five armed ships in all!

The Royal Navy, of course, had the logistics of distance to content with. It had to transport supplies all the way across the Atlantic Ocean and it had to perform the difficult task of simultaneously protecting these conveys and blockading the whole American coastline. Its commanders quarrelled amongst themselves, organisation was generally slipshod, sailors deserted and suffered diseases and the fleet was constantly under threat from the French and Spanish Navies. Yet, even after taking these disadvantages into consideration, the American Navy at its inception, still had only less than a third of the ships and less than a quarter of the armament that the Royal Navy could muster in American waters. Not surprisingly, therefore, that the chance of serving in the Continental Navy was not something that many persons considered.

For some, enlisting was thought as good as committing suicide. Members of the Patriot Party, for instance, refused commissions as officers because as they forthrightly put it, 'they did not choose to be hanged'. Meanwhile most of the experienced American seamen were perfectly happy to continue serving on 'privateers' - private armed vessels which attacked British merchant shipping for profit. In terms of self-interest, their decision is all too understandable. They made handsome money from their raids and, by avoiding full naval conflict, ran as few risks as possible, and being free of naval rule, their crews avoided the often harsh punishments meted out by Naval discipline. Arguments of the most persuasive sort would have been needed to change their minds and convince them to put up with the danger, the wet and oppressive quarters and the considerably reduced prize money for the good of the Colonies which, at that stage, was not even a society that recognized itself as a separate nation. Patriotism did not have the appeal that it later would have, and there was nobody eloquent or interested enough to plead the Navy's cause. Most seamen, as a consequence, stuck to the privateers.

The Navy's officers, such as they were, came from a merchant background and lacked both the experience and tactical expertise required for naval battles. As for the lower ranks, press gangs were an absolute necessity for supplying crews, which in themselves caused problems. As one captain lamented, the ships were too often manned by 'green country lads, many of them not clear of their sea-sickness', and they had to rely on foreign mercenaries and British prisoners of war, captured in battle, to make up the numbers.

It was in this climate that John Paul Jones considered a career with the Continental Navy. Neither related to, nor an important figure in the local community, by force of personality and experience however, he impressed the Naval Committee enough to get himself appointed First Lieutenant on 7 December 1775 with the task of helping to fit out the warship USS *Alfred*. The Continental Navy, of course, required a flag to show their opponents that they were not just pirates but a legitimate fighting force on the business of a just cause - and, ironically, John Paul Jones himself, a Scot from the land of his enemy, was the first to raise the predecessor of the 'stars and stripes' - the Grand Union flag; thirteen red and white stripes, representing the thirteen Colonies with the combined crosses of St Andrew and St George in the upper left quadrant, representing the desire for autonomy, the right for the Colonies to tax themselves without completely breaking away from the British Crown. 'I hoisted with my own hands the flag of freedom', he proudly declared and in the spring of 1776, he took part in the first sea battle of the American Navy, which unfortunately, was not a particularly glorious encounter.

Following the ignominious opening of hostilities, and to the great relief of his independent spirit, John Paul Jones was transferred and given command of the twelve gun sloop, *Providence*, which he led on a successful seven week tour of duty in the Atlantic, capturing several small vessels and disrupting the Novia Scotia fishing fleet. He repeated his success on his next tour of the Atlantic, this time as captain of the USS *Alfred*, during which time he captured four substantial British ships. Success, however, offered no protection against both the nepotism of naval appointments and the unpopularity of his style of leadership. Considered an outsider and an over-demanding taskmaster, John Paul Jones was replaced as captain of the USS *Alfred* and, for a while not given another command. In Esek Hopkin's words, 'It is impossible to man and get these vessels together and from the number of complaints I have had. . . it will be more difficult to man vessels under his command than any other officer.' Indeed, even his own crew once complained of his manner, writing in a petition of complaint that, 'his temper and treatment [of us] is insufferable'.

It was while in this state of enforced retirement, that John Paul Jones heard of an idea to form a task force that would cross the Atlantic Ocean and pin the British down in their own waters; but privateers still made it impossible for Congress to man enough boats. He longed to be a part of that grand scheme, and again through force of personality, he got himself promoted to captain and was determined to achieve single-handedly what Congress could not.

In 1777 Captain Jones was given command of the 318-ton eighteen-gun sloop, USS *Ranger*, then being fitted out at Portsmouth, New

Hampshire. A large part of the British army under General Burgoyne had just surrendered at Saratoga after a spectacular defeat and Jones was full of optimism that he would be given charge of an excellent new warship, *L'Indien*, which was being built in Amsterdam. In a mood of confidence he set sail for Europe. Unfortunately, whether because of delays in refitting, or because of pressure exerted by British partisans in Holland, Jones could not take command of *L'Indien*.

Once again experiencing a setback, John Paul Jones reached Nantes on 2 December 1777, and went to visit Paris, where Benjamin Franklin was Commissioner of the American Colonies in France. Pleading his cause to be given a task suitable to his talents, Franklin recognised in Captain Jones potential and supported his career. Eventually Jones was given a mission that could have been tailor-made for his disposition - he received orders to cruise about the British Isles and undertake a series of raids 'for distressing the enemies of the United States'. Perhaps as a perverse gesture, he set off immediately for Whitehaven and the waters where he had first taken to the sea.

The *Ranger* with a crew of 150 men, was a fast ship, ideal for lightning raids on the British coast, and Jones's plan was appropriately bold - to steal into Whitehaven harbour and destroy as much shipping in one night as the Navy might be able to destroy in a whole year of scouring the seas. He was not, however, supported by the crew in this endeavour, who preferred the suggestion of his Executive Officer, Lieutenant Thomas Simpson to attack the much safer and more profitable target of British Commerce. Once again, Captain Jones had to enforce discipline at the point of a gun and set off in one boat with twenty reluctant sailors to overcome the sentries guarding the fort at Whitehaven and spike the canons on the night of 22/23 April 1778. Meanwhile, the remainder of the crew, instead of firing the ships in the harbour went on a drinking spree, and a deserter alerted the inhabitants of the town and Jones was forced to abandoned his sorte and flee having only set fire to a few ships at anchor.

While it is undeniable that the whole debacle at Whitehaven was an unmitigated failure, with not much damage done and only twenty or so people, all on shore, even slightly injured, the shock to the local population, and indeed, the entire nation, was incalculable.

'What was done. . .' Jones himself wrote later, 'is sufficient to show that not all their boasted navy can protect their own coats' - a disagreeable lesson for any Briton to digest; defied on its own doorstep by a rebellious Colonist!

The local newspaper, the *Cumberland Packet Extraordinary*, faced with the biggest story in its history, reported the incident in the following manner:

> *Late last night or early this morning a number of armed men (to the amount of thirty) landed at this place, by two boats from an American privateer, as appears from one of the people now in custody. . . A little after 3 o'clock this morning he* [John Paul Jones] *rapped at several doors in Marlborough Street (adjoining one of the piers) and informed them that fire had been set to one of the ships in the harbour* [and] *matches were laid in several others; the whole world would soon be in a blaze, and the town also destroyed. . .*
>
> *An alarm was immediately spread, and his account proved too true. The Thompson, Captain Richard Johnson, a new vessel and one of the finest ever built here, was in a flame. It was low water, consequently all the shipping in port was in the most imminent danger and . . . as there was the greatest reason to fear that the flames would, from it, soon be communicated to the town. . . . By an uncommon exertion, the fire was extinguished. . . thus, in a providential manner,* [this action] *prevented all the dreadful consequences which might have ensued.*

He then sailed north to Kirkcudbright Bay, in Scotland, and at around 11am on 23 April landed on St Mary's Isle, a promontory stretching out into the bay, with the intention taking the Earl of Selkirk hostage who could then be traded for American sailors languishing in the British prison hulks, treated as pirates rather than prisoners of war. Unfortunately, the Earl was away, but Jones' men insouciantly intruded on the Countess of Selkirk at breakfast and sized the family silver. Later, totally mortified by his men's actions, Captain Jones bought back the silver from his crew and returned it to the Earl and Countess with an apology.

The following day, Jones set sail for Northern Ireland intent on the prize of a twenty-gun sloop, HMS *Drake*, which had been spotted on his way north. With great cunning, Jones drew the 273-ton HMS *Drake* out of Carrickfergus Bay, and off Belfast Lough, engaged the sloop in battle. The two were approximately equal in burthen and armament, but taking advantage of the wind, after a close action lasting an hour in which HMS *Drake's* rigging was cut to ribbons and her commanding officer killed, her master surrendered to John Paul Jones.

First under tow, and then under jury rig, Jones and his crew got their prize safely to Brest, a seaport in North-west France, together with 228 prisoners of war, who were exchanged for American sailors in English hulks. His reception was euphoric. Ballads were composed about the prowess of the USS *Ranger* and its heroic captain, and the reputation of the American Navy blossomed. At last, American sailors ceased to be treated as pirates and began to be feared as formidable adversaries.

John Paul Jones's activites had strikingly demonstrated the vulnerablity of the coastline and the *Morning Chronicle and London Advertiser* accompanied its report of the raid on St Mary's Isle with some distinctly sharp observations on this subject:

> *The audacious conduct of the crew of the American privateer at Whitehaven, and on the coast of Scotland, will have this good effect; it will teach our men of war on the coast station, and our cruisers in St George's Channel, to keep a more sharp look out.*
>
> *The ruinous state of the fortifications of many of our seaport towns, so likewise the open and defenceless posture of many others, at present seems to suggst some very alarming reflections. In all places like Whitehaven, the want of a necessary range of fortifications seems almost inexcusable, especially as the materials are in great plenty at or near the spot, labour cheap, etc.*

At Brest, Jones, however, was soon eager to embark on further raiding parties, and there is a sentence in one of the recruitment posters he had printed to entice crews to join his adventure that demonstrates graphically his state of mind at that time: 'I wish to have no connection with any ship that does not sail fast, for I intend to go into harm's way.' Success ought to breed success, but, as was often the case in Captain Jones's career, he was not given the command he deserved and instead of a fast warship, he was put in charge of a sluggish old 900-ton East Indiaman which the French government bought for him and renamed *Bonhomme Richard* as a compliment to Franklin. A squadron was then formed around this ship which consisted of the new 36-gun USS *Alliance*, commanded by a half-mad Frenchman in the American service named Pierre Landais; the French frigate *Pallas*; and a French corvette and cutter, all flying the American ensign. With infinite difficulty, Jones got the *Bonhomme Richard* converted, gunned, equipped and manned and on the 14 August 1779 this rag-tag squadron set sail from Lorient.

Initially, it was his intention to provide a diversion to draw attention away from a proposed joint French and Spanish invasion of the South of England, but in the end it was decided that he would seek out and destroy a British warship escorting a large number of merchantmen and capture what prizes he could.

For the first four weeks or so of his mission in late 1779, Jones led the task force round the west coast of Ireland and England and attempted some of the acts of extreme daring that had Britain trembling. In the Firth of Forth, a British private yacht approached to ask for gunpowder to defend the coast against none other than John Paul Jones himself. With typical sang froid, he acceded to their request, gathered as much information as he could about the British defences and then asked one of the yacht's crew on board to pilot him into Leith harbour where he intended to fire all the ships at anchor there.

When the yacht had pulled away, John Paul Jones nonchalantly asked the pilot what the news was. 'Why', the pilot burst out, 'that

Figure 1. A map of the sea defences of Whitby, during 1794. At that time there were twelve 18-pounder canons at the western battery (still called Battery Parade), and seven 18-pounders on the east side below St Mary's church. Two additional canons were also placed at the end of the pier.

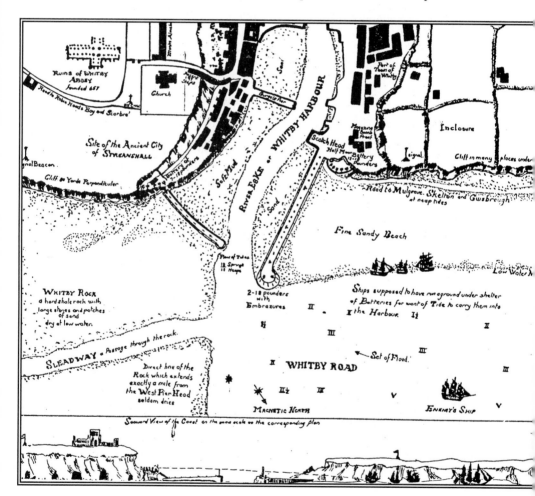

rebel and pirate Jones is off the coast and ought to be hanged'. Jones calmly replied, 'I am Paul Jones', and, as the man begged for mercy, he simply laughed and assured him that he would not be harmed. Fortunately, severe storms intervened to protect Leith; meanwhile, Landais, in command of the USS *Alliance*, was behaving ever more erratically, refusing to obey Jones's orders and going off on his own in search of prize ships, and the French cutter got lost off the Skellings and never rejoined the squadron.

John Paul Jones was less easily discouraged, and much more feared, as he began to seem unstoppable. On 20 September 1779 he appeared off Newcastle, but decided against attacking it, as his fellow-captains were eager to move on before the Royal Navy, fully aroused since his intrusion into the Firth of Forth, caught up with them. 'I have had the mortification of seeing him. . . this afternoon with three prizes. . .' wrote one irate resident of Newcastle to the Admiralty, '*and nothing in the world to oppose him.*'

He constantly threatened to plunder the ports of the northern coast, and it was said he had an especial eye to Whitby on account of its then increasing prosperity. The inhabitants of Whitby lived in a constant state of terror for a long period (Figure 1). From the situation of the town, the only hope of safety for the people in case of a raid lay in immediate flight, so that we hear of carts and wagons kept ready packed with valuables in the yards and outhouses; women kept money sewed up in their stays and in the hems of their petticoats, and they frequently slept with their jewellery on their persons, so as to be ready to start at the first note of alarm. Some of the old houses of the neighbourhood have regular built 'hidy-holes' in their grounds connected with the house by a secret passage - as, for instance, at the *Woodlands,* Sleights, and the house *Leesholme,* in Bagdale, Whitby. Humbler folk dug holes in their gardens, and secreted their treasures as best they might.

Eventually Paul Jones first appeared off Skinningrove, north of Whitby, and fired into this peaceful quarter; and his men landed in search of provisions, and it is recorded that he pillaged certain 'Larders and Cellars', but above that, not much harm was achieved. At Whitby itself, he was actually fired upon by the soldiers in charge of the Battery (Figure 2) which had been mounted on the East Cliff, above the spot where the Spa Ladder now stands. Unfortunately, the results were a disaster, for the shots failed, and a canon burst killing the gunners who were blown over the cliffs on to the rocks below.

Continuing along the East coast of Yorkshire, Captain Jones's luck held, and at sunset on 23 September 1779, Jones finally intercepted

Figure 2. One of two gunpowder stores (below) which survive from the eighteenth century western battery at Battery Parade (above).

the Baltic convoy of forty-four ships protected by HMS *Serapis* and HMS *Countess of Scarborough* off Flamborough Head.

Having made sure of the safety of the convoy which scattered to the north, the two British warships turned to engage the Americans (Figure 3). By comparison, the British craft were newer, faster, better armed and more manoeuvrable, but the American ships were slightly larger. The 20-gun sloop, the *Countess of Scarborough* gave battle to the USS *Pallas* but was quickly overcome and captured by Jones's men, while HMS *Serapis,* a 44-gun frigate under the command of Captain Richard Pearson made for Jones in the *Bonhomme Richard.* As John Paul Jones ran up the 'Stars and Stripes', the ships opened fire, unfortunately, two of Jones's 18-pounders exploded immediately, killing many of the gunners and putting his biggest guns out of action. Disadvantaged, he saw his only hope against a ship with superior speed and firepower, was to get up close and board it - an obviously risky and difficult manouvre, since the *Serapis* would be trying to keep its distance.

Both ships jockeyed for position, the British endeavouring to go broadside, Jones trying to keep them close. With supreme skill, however, Jones suddenly took advantage of a gust of wind to rush ahead of the *Serapis* and then lock the two craft together. Fastened with grappling hooks, for two hours, muzzle to muzzle, an unforgetable battle ensued. The British could not get free and the American sharpshooters high in the rigging of the *Bonhomme Richard* scoured the decks of HMS *Serapis* with grenades and gunfire. At the same time, the British 18-pounders wiped out most of the American cannons and bombarded the ship continually, thundering round after round into her shattered frame. Incredibly, to complicate matters for Jones, his own side in the form of Captain Landais, suddenly had the *Alliance* fire a broadside at the *Bonhomme Richard,* his lethal jealousy driving him to try and sink John Paul Jones and claim victory for himself!

As fires broke out across the *Bonhomme Richard* and his gunners died in large numbers, Jones himself took command of a 9-pounder on the quarterdeck. At this stage of the battle, in disbelief, he heard his chief gunner shout to the British, 'Quarter! Quarter! For God's sake!' To Jones, his ship may have been taking in water, his crew deci-

Figure 3. The battle of Flamborough Head, 1779.

mated and, for the last two hours he may have endured a firefight that would have petrified lesser men, but nothing would have induced him to surrender. Consequently, when Pearson, the commander of HMS *Serapis*, shouted back, 'Do you ask for quarter?' Jones uttered those famous words, 'I have not yet begun to fight.' This indomitable will power won the day. Firing again and again at *Serapis'* mainmast, Jones finally brought it down and Captain Pearson could stand the carnage no longer - at around 10.30pm, the British vessel with five feet of water in its hold, its mainmast, rigging and sails shot away, surrendered.

Following the engagement, the *Bonhomme Richard* was found to be in a worse state than the *Serapis* and sank two days later, nevertheless, the battle of Flamborough Head was an American victory. Jones, his men transferred to the *Serapis,* sailed both her and the *Countess of Scarborough* back to France as prizes. Five hundred and four prisoners were taken, including, 26 officers, a bitter blow for the Royal Navy. But casualties had been high on both sides, and the inevitable 'butchers bill' was evenly balanced. The *Bonhomme Richard* suffered 150 killed and wounded, almost half its complement of 322, while HMS *Serapis* acknowledged 117 killed and wounded.

'That Celebrated Seaman', as a sixpenny broadsheet described him, continued to embarrass the British government even on his return voyage to France. On 24 September 1779, the day after the battle of Flamborough Head, Lord Carlisle, wrote from his Cumberland estate: 'We have alarms here on our coast. One Paul Jones flings us all into consternation and terror and will hinder Lady Carlisle's sea bathing.' In the last week of that month the newspapers were full of reports of the recent battle and rumours of his current whereabouts, but none of the patrols sent in search of him managed to locate his position. On 1 October, the *Morning Post* commented despairingly, 'Paul Jones resembles a Jack o' Lantern, to mislead our mariners and terrify our coasts. He is no sooner seen than lost.'

He was never caught, and by 3 October Jones, with his two prizes, was safe at anchor in the Texel Roads, lying behind the island of the same name which sheltered the Zuider Zee and forms the harbour for Amsterdam. The Dutch were officially neutral, but the Hollanders made no secret of their symapthies, as a new ballad of that date confirmed:

Here comes Paul Jones, such a nice fellow!
A born American, no Englishman at all. . .
He does many bold deeds for the good of his friends.

On 12 October, one Englishman resident in Amsterdam wrote angrily to a London newspaper about the Dutch reaction to Jones's presence.

This desperado parades the streets and appears upon 'Change with the effrontery of a man of the first condition. No sooner was it known in France that he was in the Texel, than a courier was dispatched with orders for him to go overland to Paris, where he says he is to have the grant of a fresh commission and a larger squadron, sufficient to make a descent on any part of Great Britain or Ireland. . . The Dutch look upon him to be a brave officer. Nay, they even go so far as to lay odds that before Christmas he lands a force in England or Ireland.

On 27 December 1779 John Paul Jones (Figure 4) sailed from Holland for France in the USS *Alliance*. He cruised to Corunna and then back to Lorient which he reached on 19 February 1780. In mid-April Jones arrived in Paris to be greeted with a hero's welcome. His incredible triumph at the battle of Flamborough Head and his peerless heroism had become the talk of Europe. The French Emperor Louis XVI awarded him the Order of Military Merit, and the American Congress passed a vote of thanks for his service to the country. John Paul Jones was at the pinnacle of his career. 'The cry of Versailles and the clamour of Paris became as loud in favour of Monsieur Jones as of Monsieur Franklin,' wrote Benjamin Franklin himself, 'and the inclination

Figure 4. A contemporary portrait of John Paul Jones, c.1779, painted shortly after the battle of Flamborough Head.

of the ladies to embrace him almost as fashionable and as strong.' 'He is the most agreeable seawolf one could wish to meet with,' penned one enraptured Parisienne to a friend.

Yet for all his achievements and popularity, ironically, this was also to be the start of a decline in his fortunes. Jones was again refused a commission in the French Navy. Instead he was given command of the sloop *Ariel* and sent back to America with despatches. He arrived back in Philadelphia after an appallingly stormy crossing in 1781. There, Congress gave Captain Jones command of the half-built USS *America,* the only 74-gun ship in its fleet, then at Portsmouth, New

Hampshire. For a year Jones laboured hard getting the America completed, launched and fitted out, only to loose her in 1782 because Congress, unwillingly to support a peace-time navy, presented her to France as a diplomatic gesture.

Jones returned to Europe and spent a good part of the rest of his life in France going through the tiresome business of collecting prize money due to his squadron, and endeavouring without success to obtain a command in the French Navy. His last appearance in England was in 1786, when he was entertained by the City of London. It was, said one speaker forgivingly, 'better to have him at Lloyds seeking to insure his own cargoes, than at sea seeking cargoes insured by others.' Evenutally, on the recommendation of Thomas Jefferson, John Paul Jones obtained a commission in the Imperial Russian Navy, as Rear Admiral commanding a squadron of nine frigates on the Liman of the Dnieper, where Russia was trying to capture Ochakov from the Turks.

The Russian Black Sea Fleet was a scratch collection of shoal draft vessels manned by impressed serfs, Cossacks, Volga boatmen, and Levantine pirates, officered in part by adventurers and mercenaries from six or seven nations. The Russian Empress Catherine felt that only an outstanding naval officer from another country could weld this motley collection into a real fighting force. Undoubtedly Jones could have achieved this aim had he not got into the ill graces of Prince Potemkin, the commander-in-chief, who unaccountably resented having yet another foreign flag officer on his hands.

In spite of all the intrigues, however, Jones fought the Turks and won the two battles of the Liman in June 1788 - shoal water fights in a narrow estuary with little space to deploy and manouvre between mudflats. Unfairly, Prince Nassau-Siegen, commander of the light flotilla of landing craft, got all the credit from Potemkin, and Jones was left out of the battle honours - nevertheless, though, he won the respect and loyalty of the Russian naval officers under him, but that did not help his situation with the commander-in-chief and possibly inflamed Potemkin's jealousy, who relieved Jones and sent him to St Petersburg to await orders.

Jones waited at St Petersburg through the winter of 1788-9. In the spring Kontradmiral Pavel Ivanovich Jones was falsely accused of rape through the intrigues of an important personage, probably Nassau-Siegen; shortly afterwards, this same Prince, who had charmed the Empress, received command of her Baltic Fleet, which post Jones had been led to anticipate for himself. Embittered, he left Russia, and after travelling through central Europe, returned to France to settle down in May 1790 in a pleasant apartment at 19 Rue de Tournon, in Paris, where the French Revolution prevented any further adventures.

Jones spent most of his time writing letters to every influential person of his acquaintance seeking a naval or diplomatic postion; and his importunity was finally rewarded by two commissions from President George Washington, dated 1 and 2 June 1792, appointing him American Consul in Algeria and Plenipotentiary to negotitate with the Dey for the release of American prisoners. Unfortunately, it was too late. On 18 July 1792, aged forty-five, just weeks before these commissions reached him in France, John Paul Jones, died from an attack of bronchial pneumonia, following a bout of jaundice and nephritis.

He was buried at the expense of the French Assemblee Legislative in an unmarked grave in the Protestant Cemetery on the Rue de Granges-aux-Belle. A hundred years later, in 1905, the lead coffin was exhumed, and the body identified and carried back to the United States in an American crusier, escorted by three others, and met off Nantucket Shoals by seven battleships. He was brought to Annapolis, in Maryland, where he was laid to rest in a marble sarcophagus in the crypt of the Naval Academy chapel, an institution which his example had done so much to help establish.

Bibliography

John Paul Jones. Reprint from *Lloyd's Evening Post,* Monday 27 April to Wednesday 29 April 1778, Vol.XLII, No.3552, Friends of Whitehaven Museum, 1977.

Battle between the Bon Homme Richard and the Serapis, Old South Leaflet No.152, Directors of the Old South Work, Boston, n.d., re-issued by Whitehaven Museum and Art Gallery, n.d.

History of John Paul Jones, The Pirate (pamphlet), Glasgow, n.d., re-issued by Whitehaven Museum and Art Gallery, n.d.

Longmate, Norman *Island Fortress - The Defence of Great Britain 1603-1945.* Hutchinson, 1991.

O'Brien, Giles *World Famous War Heroes.* Parragon, n.d.

Jeffrey, Percy Shaw *Whitby Lore and Legend.* Horne and Son, Whitby, 1923 reprinted Caedmon Press, 1985, 1991.

Kemp, Peter (editor) *The Oxford Companion to Ships and the Sea.* OUP, 1976.

Morison, Samuel Eliot *John Paul Jones,* 1959.

3. Now Showing – The Cinemas of Bridlington

by David Wright

FOR MANY OF US IN THE 1950s AND 1960s a visit to the cinema was a twice weekly occurrence (Figure 1). Yet even at that period its popularity was on the decline, brought on with the advent of television. The heyday of film was in the 1920s and 1930s and during these two decades picture houses sprang up in profusion. Indeed, it was not uncommon for towns to have five, six or more purpose-built cinemas as well as other venues converted to show animated films. Even relatively small villages and suburbs often boasted at least one picture house. Bridlington, a seaside resort built onto a fishing village down toward the lower end of the East Coast of Yorkshire, was no exception, and at one time could claim to have at least five cinemas operating simultaneously.

The old Roxy cinema on Quay Road (Figure 2), nowadays boarded-up and almost totally ignored by passers-by only too used to its unattended presence, was once a focal point in the entertainment of the people of the old Town. If attendance at the downtown Winter Gardens, Lounge or Regal cinemas on a Saturday afternoon cost ninepence, then at the Roxy it would be a mere 'tanner' (six old pence), a sum well within the grasp of most Saturday matinee devotees.

Figure 1. Queuing to visit the cinema in the 1950s to see *Aint Misbehavin*.

Figure 2. The Roxy cinema as it stood in July 1998 with its decorative facarde. *Photograph by Alan Whitworth*

Formerly a Temperance Hall, in what was then St John's Street, it was bought in 1912 by a Mr Freeman and transformed into a picture house. He called his new acquisition the Picturedrome. In 1913 the Picturedrome was advertising the screening of the *Battle of Gettysberg*. Around 1918 the cinema changed ownership and became the property of a Mr A Lawton. The manager in 1921 was a Mr J Beanland; in 1933 it was a Frederick M Harrop. At that time admission prices had risen from five pence to sixpence, with the most expensive seat rising from ninepence to one shilling.

In April 1930 the cinema was advertised in the local press as 'The completely renovated Adelphi Picture Theatre', with a new screen, British Eastern Electric Talking machines, and was about to show the cinema's first talkie, *Broadway Melody*. The name Adelphi, however, lasted for only four years, and around 1935 the name of the cinema changed to the Roxy and had four hundred seats.

A bold facade erected over the original building announced both Coming Attractions and displayed 'stills' of the films Now Showing. Hordes of local Saturday afternoon cinemagoers, most of who were aged under sixteen years old, took in supplies at Hooper's shop next door before entering the Roxy; bubble-gum, gobstoppers, aniseed balls, 'Black Jacks' and other 'five-a-penny' oddments. Others, of course, in order to emulate the character of their favourite screen stars would sneak in illicit packets of Woodbines or Park Drive cigarettes, or even the cheaper brands Four Dominoes (Price 6d) or Single Joystick (Price 6d) a veritable six inch clothespole of a cigarette.

On entering the cinema, a ticket was purchased from Mrs Britzmann at the pay desk in the foyer, after which, new members of the audience were led by Mrs Thompson, the usherette, to their individual seats spotlit in the darkened cinema by Mrs Thompson's accurately-aimed torchbeam. The seats at the Roxy, unlike most other picture houses, sloped upwards from the back of the auditorium towards the screen, a reversal to the usual arrange-ment. The toilets here, were situated through an exit door to the side of the cinema in an outside enclosed passageway. If it rained heavily, an umbrella was a near-necessity for anyone wishing to answer the call of nature.

The Roxy cinema went under the various affectionate titles of Bug House, Flea Pit and Ranch House, over which supervision and total control was held by sheriff Jim Thompson.[1] To maintain order in an always disorderly house, he would often become a cane-weilding tyrant, whacking his cane against the back of an empty seat, the sound of which would occasion an immediate cinema-wide hush! Illicit cigarettes in the mouths of obviously underage smokers were whipped out from between unsuspecting lips with one deft flick of this instrument. Such was his fearsome reputation, that if Jim had been a gunslinger, then like the name of one of the films of the era, he would have been unquestionably The Fastest Gun Alive.

On the retirement of Mr Thompson, he was replaced by a certain sheriff Vasey, a tall portly man whose wife (his deputy) was in build similar but in height quite the opposite. The couple had a more artistic opinion of what films should be screened, consequently, in the eyes of the local youth, the quality of films diminished. Audience control at the Roxy during this period was also maintained by the use of monitors who ruled not by their power of persuasion, but with clenched fists.

One of the main features of the Saturday afternoon matinee was the ubiquitous serial featuring Flash Gordon, Zorro, or some such hero; where each week he fell headlong to certain death over a sheer precipice, only to be found the following week averting disaster by clinging to a cliff-top tree having been seen in the previous episode clearly plunging hundreds of feet after the heroine, who was now also found miraculously clinging to an adjacent branch.

At the time of the onset of the Second World War, the Roxy was owned by A J Spinks of Hull (who had also briefly owned the People's Palace). During the years from 1941 to 1945 the cinema was requisitioned by the Ministry of Defence for wartime storage and closed. After the war in the late-1940s, Messrs Harrison and Vasey reopened the Roxy which now had 497 seats. Admission prices at this date ranged from one shilling to 2s 4d. By the beginning of the 1950s Mr G H Vasey, mentioned above, was the sole owner of the cinema.

In the late-fifties and early-sixties the Roxy, already beginning to feel the winds of change, began to feature after the evening screenings in an attempt to keep up audience interest, a three-piece musical combo known as the *Roxy Revellers*. The leader of this combo was a Mr Jarvis, whose real occupation was running a newsagents. Local budding talent mimicking Sinatra, Johnny Ray, Elvis or Cliff Richard, accompanied by the strains of the combo, would encourage with their vocal performances, an audience reaction from suppressed groans to outright laughter.

After the time of the Roxy Revellers came the period of the late-night tombola sessions which heralded the demise of the buildings use as a cinema. Not long after, the picture house was converted to an outright Bingo Hall. After a further two years providing bingo-only, the Roxy eventually closed its doors for good.

Today, without the pedestrian crossing situated outside what were in the 1950s the shops of Charter's, Fish and Chip emporium and George Lonsdale's, Barber, it is impossible to cross the busy Quay Road for the volume of traffic. If this had been the case almost half a century ago, then most of the young thigh-slapping, play-acting Zorro's and Lone Ranger's galloping straight out of the Roxy cinema after a Saturday afternoon matinee heading for 'them thar hills' somewhere beyond the bushes in the park across the road opposite, with school raincoats buttoned-up like capes around their necks, with neither a glance left or right for traffic; and if the volume of cars had been as nowadays, most of these wannabe hero's would have been flattened to oblivion beneath the wheels of oncoming vehicles.

The Roxy was never fitted for Cinemascope due to the narrowness of the building. The last film to be screened at the venue, on Monday 30 October 1961, was *Kim* starring Errol Flynn, supported by *White Warrior* and *A Question of Loyalty.*

On Thursday, 2 July 1938, the opening programme for the then recently-constructed Regal on the Promenade, described the venue as a 'new luxury cinema'. The opening performance was scheduled to begin at 7.30pm, and consisted of (1) The opening ceremony performed by the Mayor of Bridlington, Councillor J W Robson, JPCC, and his wife, with the Deputy Mayor and Mayoress in attendance in the presence of the Chairman and Managing Director of the new cinema Mr Louis Morris and the General Manager, Wally Braisford (2) Claire Trevor and Donald Woods starring in *Big Town Girl* (3) Florence de Jong at the magnificent British Compton Organ (4) forthcoming presentations and the British Paramount News (5) John Barrymore and John Howard in *Bulldog Drummond Comes Back* (6) God Save the King.

The auditorium had seating for 1,500 people, and the building incorporated four lock-up shops and a spacious restaurant with blush-tinted mirrors, an orchestra platform, and a polished oak floor for dancing. Cinema opening times were advertised as, 'Doors Open 1.45pm' and then 'continuous performances from 2.00pm through until 10.30pm.' Seat prices were Front Stalls, ninepence;[2] Rear Stalls, 1s 0d and 1s 3d; Rear Circle, 1s 3d and 1s 6d; Front Circle, two shillings. A monthly magazine was available post-free to cinemagoers who left their name and address at the box office.

The cinema interior had been designed by Eugene Mollo and Michael Egan, well-known London cinema designers. The structure had been built by Messrs Leightons, of Potters Bar, Middlesex and Victoria Street, London, who had constructed many other picture houses up and down the country. The entire building itself had been planned by C Edmund Wilford, ARIBA, of Eagle House, Jermyn Street, London, designer and architect of some of the best-known contemporary theatres and cinemas of the day. The auditorium was air-conditioned, and the electrical installations were at the vanguard of the 1930s cinema technology with great plaster grills surrounding the interior. The fibrous plasterwork had been installed by W J Wilson and Son, of Mansfield.

Florence de Jong, the resident Regal organist, was of worldwide renown, and was a popular BBC Radio performer and West End star. She had been a pianist since the age of eight, and an organist since fifteen, and had been the first female Wurlitzer organist in Britain.

Her first appointment had been at Terry's Theatre in the Strand, London, at the age of fourteen. She had played there for a salary of twenty-five shillings a week, but had eventually been dismissed because of her young age, and the fact that the theatre-cum-cinema occasionally screened 'Adults Only' films. Her signature tune was *Passing Thoughts.* The daughter of the composer Con Baga, Florence married popular orchestra leader and composer, Harry de Jong.

The Regal cinema organ at the time of the opening was manufactured by the John Compton Company, of London, organ-builders with an international reputation. It had an illuminated console operated by the organist who could control the coloured lights sweeping the bodywork of the instrument.

By the 1950s the Regal cinema had been acquired by the ABC cinema group, and a number of subtle changes occurred. The expansive foyer area now displayed life-size cardboard replicas of the stars of 'Coming Attractions'. Also featured was a well-stocked confectionary and tobacco kiosk adjacent to the pay desk. A smartly-uniformed commissionaire patrolled the area, organising the queues which, at the height of the summer season, snaked out through the swing-doors, along the front of the cinema and down a side alley which ran the full length of the building. The approach to the auditorium was down a long corridor whose walls were hung with black and white photographs of the big cinema stars of that and previous eras. The *ABC Film Guide,* price sixpence, was also sold in this area.[3]

The new ABC Regal was both now impressive and well-organised, however, in some respects its reluctance to move with the times (possibly a fault with the entire ABC organisation) ensured it missed out in some areas and failed, for instance, to screen most of the early youth-oriented films and the first Cinemascope film entitled, *The Robe.*[4] Yet despite this lack of foresight, the Regal under its new management, did hold the monopoly on Saturday morning entertainment in the ABC Minors Club, or just known as the 'Minors' to those children in attendance.

A boon for parents, especially mother's, who could leave their offspring for an hour or two in complete safety and go off and undertake the weekly shopping, the Saturday morning screenings consisted of a feature film, usually a poor and hopeless B-Movie, a serial, a comedy feature (mostly starring the Three Stooges or the Bowery Boys) and a liberal scattering of *Looney Tunes and Merry Melody* cartoons. The precursor to Saturday morning children's television, the ABC Minors were immensely popular in their time.

Like the Roxy cinema, the audience was controlled by a posse of monitors, but at the ABC, monitors wore identification badges in their school blazer lapels and were a less violent bunch than those at the Ranch House. Here, they preferred to operate a 'snitch' policy, informing against delinquents to the cinema staff of any infringement of 'the rules'.

During the interval at the ABC Minors Saturday morning shows, after the communal singing of the Minors anthem accompanied by the bouncing ball, which started:

We are the boys and girls well-known as the Minors of the ABC;
And every Saturday all line up
To see the films we like and shout aloud with glee...

Members of the audience who had had a birthday in the previous week, were welcomed onto the stage by the cinema manager, who presented them with a free pass for the following Saturday performance. Some of these claimants, however, often attempted to obtain free passes at more frequent intervals, but were usually spotted and given a stern lecture by the manager in front of the entire cinema audience.

This behaviour brings to mind a story of a similar action which took place at the Spa Royal Hall (Figure 3) in 1962, during a one-off amateur variety spectacular entitled *The Senior Service Show*, sponsored by the manufacturers of the Senior Service cigarette. The compere of the show was a young and slim Bill Maynard, undoubtedly down on his luck, who introduced each amateurish act

Figure 3. Spa Royal Hall and Promenade in the 1950s. *From the collection of A. Whitworth*

with inflated enthusiasm as though he were announcing a Sinatra, Great Houdini, or Dame Margo Fonteyn.

The one-night show had two performances in the evening, during which, in the interval most of the adolescent audience hid in the toilets and, at the sound of the opening fanfare to the second house, reclaimed their former seats and in doing so denied many of the people queuing outside the opportunity to see the second performance. Inside, Bill, as perceptive in real-life as his later character, 'Greengrass' in *Heartbeat,* scanned the rows of teenage faces and commented drily. . . There's some familiar faces in here tonight!

Eventually, the ABC Regal cinema, like the Roxy, also succumbed to the joint onslaught of television and prize bingo. Numbered then were the days of the Pearl & Dean advertisements, an unsung artform themselves. Never again would compliant audiences be coaxed into community singing during the intermission whilst the lightning-fingered Hammond organ player rose like Dracula from beneath the stage-level, thrilling audiences with renditions of popular tunes whose lyrics were displayed on screen and adorned with quivering crochets and quavers while a bouncing ball emphasised each word; indeed, the end of the Regal in Bridlington, was the end of an era in local cinema entertainment.

The Winter Gardens first opened as the Colosseum cinema on Easter Monday, 19 April 1922, with the screening of the silent film *The Sign of the Door,* starring Norma Talmadge. A resident orchestra played dramatic music to accompany the action, and also entertained the audience during the intermission (Figure 4).

The Colosseum at that time was referred to as a 'super cinema' and had a seating capacity of just over one thousand seats. The first manager was a Mr C W Hunter who had come from the Morecambe Tower. He was later replaced by Mr F Sayer. Beside the cinema auditorium, the building housed a stage and ballroom in the basement. The printed programme for the ballroom for the week commencing 11 September 1922 advertised the following sequence of dances in what was, at that particular date, the Cecil Lennox Carnival Week - a selection of Waltzes, Fox Trot, One-Step, Chottische, Valetta, Lancer, and a final medley performed (and danced to) at fifteen minute intervals throughout the evening.

In common with other cinemas of the period, the Colosseum changed programmes twice weekly, and for the week commencing 11 September 1922, the cinema had the following programme on offer; Monday to Wednesday (1) *March* (2) *I'd Like to Fall Asleep and*

Figure 4. The Piccadilly Orchestra outside the door of the Winter Gardens in 1939. Playing at the cinema that week was May Miles Minter in Tillie and Constance Talmadge in *Her Sister from Paris.*

wake Up (3) *Topical Budget* (4) *Midnight Marriage* (5) *In My Mammy's Arms* (Song Picture) (6) *Trying to Get Along* (7) *Nomads of the North*. . . Thursday to Saturday (1) *March* (2) *Topical Budget* (3) *Loose Lions* (4) *The Bohemian Girl.*[5] The programme also invited the audience to visit the Colosseum Cafe. For the week beginning Monday 18 September, the Colosseum advertised a screening of the following four films, *The Scarlet Lady, Christie Johnston, Colorado,* and a *Tale of Two Worlds,* with the added bonus that patrons could purchase ices, cigarettes, chocolates and coffee from the attendants.

Unfortunately, within two years things began to go amiss for those managing the Colosseum, and, in 1924 a new company, The Winter Gardens (Bridlington) Limited was formed with capital amounting to £7,000 raised in one pound shares, and with a fresh Board of Directors.

In 1925 the name Winter Gardens came into general use, and while the new 'talkies' were becoming popular in most cinemas throughout the country, the Winter Gardens continued to show silent films for some time as committments inherited from the previous management were honoured. By the year 1929 the basement ballroom had become a Roller Rink as the new craze for roller-skating swept through the land. In 1930 a Western Electric Sound System was installed in the cinema, and the Winter Gardens began to show the latest talking movies; in January of that year the first sound film *The Singing Fool* starring Al Jolson was screened. The film attracted large crowds and played until mid-March. The next sound film featured at the cinema was *Say it With Songs,* an 'all talking, all singing Vitaphone Picture.' The picture house began to describe itself as 'The Winter Gardens Super Sound Cinema.

The Roller Rink, however, soon turned out to be a financial disaster, and the basement was transformed as a consequence into a Billiard Saloon, or, as it was to be eventually referred to by the clientele, the Bash Hall. It was a dingy venue presided over in the late-fifties and early-sixties by the dour, determined, deadpan, and dedicated (to the job at hand) Les, who operated the table lights from the sanctuary of his dual-function pay office and confectionary and tobacco kiosk. Any table misdemeanours such as damage to the green baize, was greeted by a frantic flashing of the table lights by the outraged proprietor to draw attention to the act, whose pipe inhalation at such times increased and transformed his already pale, subterranean complexion to a marble vampire tone. Persistent offenders were banned sine die from future admittance.

The snooker hall was situated at a significant depth below ground level, and there was only one staircase entrance up which no-one could have possibly escaped should there have been a serious fire. Some of the more frequent clients became reasonably proficient at the game, but the interest generated by television exposure to the modern game was non-existant in those days, and a one-four-seven break was about as hopeful as a modern-day multi-million pound Lottery windfall. The hall also contained a row of table tennis tables and a small Russian billiards table.

In winter months the saloon was frequented by elderly, and for the most part, refugees from the Old Town Union Workhouse. These refugees from the 'Grubber' as it was often unceremoniously referred to, would occupy the side benches of the hall on cold Sunday afternoons when the Public Library Reading Room and the Woolworths store was closed. The youth of the town at this time, sought their own particular Sunday afternoon sanctuary over the road at the Grand Pavilion 'Sunday Rendevous' whose master of ceremonies, adopting an American mode of patter, conducted a series of games and competitions whilst clapping an invitation to the audience to join in the unifying chant, 'Hey Bop a Be-Bop'.

In the cinema, the talking films soon put paid to the occasional dramatic performance formerly staged at the cinema-cum-theatre; nevertheless, the six backstage dressing rooms were retained. Cinema prices at the Winter Gardens in the mid-1930s ranged from between ninepence to two shillings. During the war years the cinema temporarily closed for business in line with Ministry of Defence directives, but soon reopened its doors again for the showing of Public Information Films including, in 1941, one on the effects of bombings. There were Sunday performances too, during the war years, for the benefit of off-duty servicemen, but by the 1950s these had been reduced to screenings from five o'clock onwards. At this time, Mr Brindley Evans (of Hull Cinemas) was booking films for the now-continuous shows whose seat prices cost from one shilling to 2s 9d. By 1956 the Panoramic Cinemascope screen had arrived, described as being thirty feet in width and fourteen feet high. The seating arrangement at this date was reduced to two less than a thousand seats to accommodate the increased screen area.

Figure 5. The Victoria Rooms Theatre and cinema at the beginning of the twentieth century.

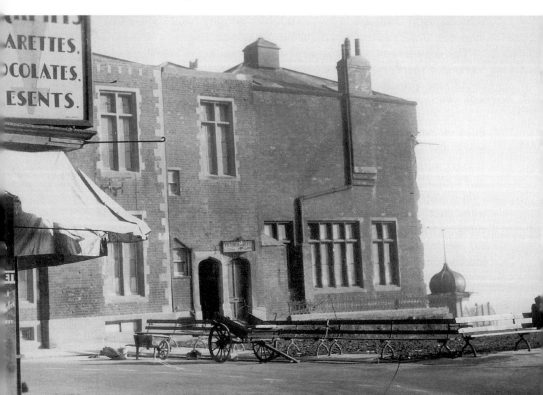

The Winter Gardens continued as a viable business enterprise through until the 1970s. Eventually, however, the video boom sounded the death knell, and closure of the cinema was finally announced by Mr Ray Hines, the manager, in February 1982. By this time it had, unfortunately, been open for only two days per week. The last films to be screened were *Adventures of a Private Eye* (X-cert) and *Cherry, Harry and Rachel* (X-cert).

Finally, before demolition in the early years of this decade, a BMX bike track was briefly opened in the empty cinema, but soon ceased to operate leaving a derelict shell.

From 1910 onwards animated pictures were screened at the Victoria Rooms, situated on the harbour top (Figure 5). The film of the *Glover Boxing Match* was very popular at the time, as were the films *Quo Vadis, Les Miserables* and *Satan,* all screened at the Victoria during the year 1913. The Victoria Rooms had seating for six hundred persons at that time, and the manager was a Mr Charles Palmer. He booked the films, actors (if required for live performances) and was responsible for the general management of the venue. In 1922 the Victoria ran one screening each evening, with a change of programme twice weekly. Admission prices at the time were from between five pence and one shilling, somewhat cheaper by comparision to other cinemas at that date.

In 1923 the Victoria Rooms ceased to screen films and concentrated on operating as a traditional live theatre. Sadly, on Friday, 22 September 1933 the building burnt to the ground. At that date it was said to have been the oldest entertainment venue in the East Riding, being over one hundred years old.

The People's Palace, formerly situated behind Prospect Street, was built in 1896. The Palace had seating for 1,500 persons. Its history and fortunes were chequered; by 1910 it had passed, initially, into the hands of the Local Council; and then on 5 August that year, it came under the management of a Mr W S Grafton, under whose guiding hand it prospered, screening such popular offerings as Beethoven's, *Moonlight Sonata* and *A Duel in the Air.* A matinee was presented every Saturday afternoon.

After 1912, the number of seats at the People's Palace was officially declared as totalling eight hundred. Soon after this date a Mr J Austin took over management of the cinema, and among the screenings he booked was the popular contemporary films *Honour Thy Father, His Life's Blood* and *At Hand's Grip with Death.* Admission prices ranged from four pence upwards to ninepence.

The *Kinematograph Yearbook* for 1922 listed the cinema as the

Palace Picture House, giving the owners at that date as Messrs Buck, Hollingworth and Luxton, and under the daily management of Mr James Winspeare. There were now three matinees each week, but only one evening performance. Interestingly, and possibly somewhat ironically, church services were held in the cinema on Sunday evenings as Sunday screenings were not allowed for many years. Admission prices had risen by this period to between sixpence and one shilling.

One of the first sound films to be screened at the Palace was entitled *Such Men Are Dangerous* starring Elinor Glynns. The date was 30 August 1930. The sound system fitted at the Palace was a British Acoustic. In the summer season the performances ran continuously from 2.30pm, and in the winter months from 6.30pm, with one daily matinee. The auditorium now sat 724 persons, and

Figure 6. The New Spa Theatre and Promenade in the late nineteenth century.

seat prices had risen to between seven pence and 1s 4d. The manager was now a Mr Henry Pocock.

In January 1940, six months after the declaration of war with Germany, the Picture Palace closed down temporarily to reopen on 27 May under the auspices of Mr A Spinks, but this was a short-lived reprieve and it closed a few months later on 23 August 1940. It was the end of the road for the People's Palace, and with the opening of the new 'super cinemas' the venue was relegated to the annals of cinema history.

Over the years the combined forces of the weather, rising damp from neglect and pigeons inhabiting the exposed roof rafters slowly rendered the building derelict. The interior of the shell was littered with a mixture of collapsed roofing material and pigeon droppings which had fallen onto the once plush seating. The cinema was eventually demolished, and the site is nowadays a car park.

In November 1912 Messrs Field and Company opened a picture house within their Oriental Lounge Complex, which was known as

the Lounge cinema. In 1914 the building was closed for refurbishment, and on its opening the first film to be screened was *The Beauty and the Bargee*. Talking films were first introduced at the Lounge in January 1913, the first entitled *The Trespasser* starring Gloria Swanson.

During the 1930s there was a fire at the Lounge. After the fire a Western Electric Wide Ranging Sound System replaced the former installation destroyed by the fire. At this date the cinema came under the ownership of the Esplanade Cafe Ltd, and had seating for 986 persons. Summer admission prices were from one shilling to 1s 4d. By the mid-1950s the cinema could boast a screen twenty feet wide and twelve feet high, but in order to accomodate this new wide-

Figure 7. The Grand Pavilion and New Terraces in the nineteenth century which housed a cinema.

Figure 8. A portrait of Norma Talmadge (*b.* 1897) from a cigarette card issued by W D & H O Wills.

screen seating had been reduced to only 855 seats priced between 1s 9d and three shillings.

The Lounge cinema stopped showing films on 28 October 1961; the final screening was *Double Bunk* featuring Ian Carmichael. For a period dancing at the Lounge, which had always alternated with the showing of films, continued, and for a brief spell in 1981, there was a programme of wrestling staged in the building.

Notes and References

1. No relation to Mrs Thompson, the usherette, as far as I am aware.
2. This price of ninepence remained static for twenty-five years or so.
3. The *ABC Film Guide* was later renamed the *ABC Film Review*.
4. This was shown at the nearby Winter Gardens.
5. *The Bohemian Girl* was voted the Picture of the Year, and was the British film of that title, not to be confused with the 1936 Laurel and Hardy picture of the same name.

4. WISH YOU WERE HERE! THE 1883 HOLIDAY JOURNAL OF GEORGE EATON OF NORWICH

Edited by Andrew White

A MANUSCRIPT PRESERVED in the Norfolk Record Office gives us an insight into a visit to Whitby more than a century ago and shows us what activities a sensible middle-class family of that period would expect to undertake while on their month's summer holiday.

The manuscript was written by George Clayton Eaton of Norwich.[1] He was one of three sons of Thomas Damant Eaton and trained at the Royal Academy, studying under Alfred Stevens. He never became a professional artist, however, having a private income. He was, nevertheless, one of the group which established the Museum in Norwich Castle, opened in 1894, and he contributed the section on pictures to the first catalogue of the Museum, published by Jarrolds in 1895. He died on 25 June 1900 at his home, *Cleveland House*, Newmarket Road, Norwich.

George Eaton came to Whitby in June and July 1883 with his family - his wife Polly, his son Frederic Ray 'Fred' and his daughter Florence Mary 'Fotty'. They stayed with Mrs Clifford, at 6 South Terrace on the West Cliff.

The Norfolk Record Office has seventeen more such holiday diaries kept by George Eaton, ranging in date from 1848 to 1895 and in compass from Scotland to Snowdonia, including the Lake District, London, the Isle of Wight, Devon and Cornwall.[2] Eaton was born in 1834 and at the time of his visit to Whitby was aged forty-nine. He was a knowledgeable and interested traveller, as can be seen from his comments upon geology, monastic remains and other features in the landscape.

Typically, the holiday was based upon Whitby - presumably for the children's sake - but with numerous family outings to other places, often by rail, including Robin Hood's Bay, Scarborough, Runswick and Staithes, and with a number of solitary trips to the waterfalls of Goathland, Roseberry Topping and even as far afield as Rievaulx and Fountains Abbeys.

Quite apart from the intrinsic interest of this journal the date coincides more or less with the period of production of those well-known images of Whitby by the photographer Frank Meadow

A VIKING ON MODERN FASHION.

"WHAT DOES T'LASS WANT WI' YON *BOOSTLE* FOR? IT AREN'T BIG ENOUGH TO *SMOGGLE* THINGS, AND SHE CAN'T *STEER* HERSELF WI' IT

Figure 1. George Du Maurier cartoon. *Courtesy of Punch*

Sutcliffe and by the *Punch* cartoonist George du Maurier. Sutcliffe was a native of the town but du Maurier only became acquainted with Whitby through a series of family holidays in the 1880s and 1890s where he stayed firstly at 1 St Hilda's Terrace, then latterly, at 9 Broomfield Terrace, Bagdale. Interestingly, Sutcliffe, for all his alleged realism, attempted to blot out entirely the summer visitors in favour of the earthy peasant qualities of the native fishing people. Du Maurier, on the other hand, liked to contrast the two (Figure 1). It is doubtful if Eaton and his family appear in any Punch cartoons because du Maurier tended to take his holidays later in the year, usually September. Nonetheless, there are many smart visitors to be seen in the backgrounds of his cartoons, braving the sights (and smells!) of the piers and harbours from the safety of their West Cliff lodgings, just like the Eatons (Figure 2).

I am particularly grateful to Captain Thomas Eaton, OBE, TD,

Figure 2. The Viqueens of Whitby. George Du Maurier. *Courtesy of Punch*

DL the present-day head of the family, both for his permission to publish the holiday journal of his grandfather and for useful background information on the Eaton family.

In editing the manuscript I have taken the liberty of expanding contractions in the text, adding a certain amount of punctuation and breaking up long paragraphs, all in the interests of readability for a modern audience. From internal evidence in the text it is clear that George Eaton did not write up his journal each day, but took the opportunity of days spent locally in Whitby to catch up on lengthier entries to do with his longer expeditions.

[June 19th Tuesday]. . . On reaching Whitby we left our luggage at the station and walked into the town to get lodgings. This hateful business was got over at last and we settled upon Mrs Clifford's, 6 South Terrace, West Cliff - a sitting room and two bedrooms for thirty-five shillings per week - a bed for Fred and a crib for Fotty being put into our room.[3] The first impression of Whitby was by no means favourable. Before we could get lodgings the emptiness of the visitors' part was depressing and no sooner had we settled on them, and before we could get in, the rain came on and lasted for about an hour. After this the weather was cold and gloomy and as Whitby is not the cleanest of places, we felt that it must have been very much overrated (Figure 3).

In the evening I took a turn by myself. I went up the 199 steps to the churchyard and the old church and along the edge of the cliff and on the West Pier.

[June 20th Wednesday] In the morning we went on the beach - that is to say the West beach which forms one long sweep of sand stretching for about three miles from the West pier of Whitby to Sandsend where the cliff runs out into the headlands. Over the sandy beach rise cliffs of reddish clay with sandstone cropping out in places on the beach. The wind was easterly and bitterly cold - the day grey and the whole scene gloomy. In the afternoon we went into some jet shops and into a workshop where two men were making jet ornaments.[4] It is very dirty work. The younger of the two was copying a head by using a sharp knife for cutting the jet, which he did by eye.

In the evening I walked by myself on the East side of the river, mounting the 199 steps which lead up the East cliff to the churchyard. This churchyard has a curious effect from the other side of the river. The Whitby people of former times seem literally to be

Figure 3. Whitby from Larpool, 1889, showing the railway line leading into the town.

laid on the shelf. There is no wall on the edge of the cliff but the grounds bend over in a green slope. The graves stand thick on the level top and one cannot help thinking that in time as the cliff crumbles away they must empty their contents into the sea, or river rather, above which in fact they stand.

Bands of sandstone crop out below the green slope, however, so that as the cliff has lasted for many ages, doubtless it will last for many ages still. I walked beyond the Abbey and on the edge of the cliffs which are here lofty and sheer down, striped with horizontal bands of stone. When the tide is in the sea breaks at their base. The country here is bleak, swelling up to a long ridge, the first step of the moors. The whole ground in sight, however, cultivated but without trees. Farm houses dotted about. A more mountainous ridge higher up the Esk valley is evidently moorland. I got on a road for a time and was surprised to find a paved footpath - slabs of stone laid crosswise. I found afterwards that these paths are common here.[5] Went as far as two lighthouses and returned by the edge of the cliffs. The coast had a grim look like the place and country.

[June 21st Thursday] In the morning on the beach and West Cliffs. These are lower than those on the East side of the river. The walk on them is very pleasant and seats are dotted about. The sun broke out today and gave things a different look. In the afternoon we went to Robin Hood's Bay - hiring a 'machine' for the trip.[6] The distance is six miles. The road lies over the bare country I walked in yesterday. On reaching the other side of the high ground, however it descends to the bay through very different scenery.

The view of the bay and the great semicircle of green cultivated and wooded slopes from the moors down to it is beautiful especially with the effects of sun and shade we saw passing over it. At the other side of the bay is a grim headland called Peak running out from a great hill the top and sides of which were evidently moorland. Our machine stopped at the top of a very steep hill which leads down through the village to the beach. We walked down and were very pleased with the 'bay town'. It is picturesque and clean and stands on both sides of a gully and immediately on the beach most curiously. On our return the driver pointed out the two stones in fields said to mark the places where Robin Hood's and Little John's arrows fell when they showed their shooting powers at Whitby Abbey.[7] The Abbey, by the by, is visible for miles around but owing to its position on the cliff has not the beauty which one would expect as it was a really beautiful building. Indeed, the general grimness which so much struck us at first applies to the ruins as well as the town, coast and country. In the evening I took Fred up the 199 steps.

[June 22nd Friday] In the morning we took the train to Glaisdale, a station up the Esk valley line. Here we saw the famous 'Beggar's Bridge' (Figure 4), which indeed can be seen from the train as it is just below it. The bridge is very elegant crossing the river by a single fine arch as is the manner among hill streams which are subject to such violent and sudden floodings. The bridge is narrow, and its date appears from a stone in the parapet to be 1619.[8]

From the bridge we walked through Arncliffe Woods by one of the paved paths common here. The scenery was very beautiful, the beauty of the wood being increased by grey masses of sandstone rock which break out among the trees. Here and there as the path rises fine views down the river can be had from the edge of the broken ground and the river itself is seen flowing among great stones. Beyond the wood the path ends in a lane which leads down to Egton Bridge. Here the views were equally beautiful but of a different kind. Being at a considerable height we saw the beauty of the valley and the smaller glens opening into it to much greater advantage than from a lower level. The

Figure 4. Beggar's Bridge, Glaisdale. *Photograph by A Whitworth*

green slopes of the little glen by which we descended with its fields and woods and the brown moorland breaking down into them were very delightful and then the stream flowing from the hills was full of great stones over which the water broke in true mountain fashion. At Grosmont we took the train again. Close by the station are some iron works and great heaps of refuse.[9]

In the afternoon the weather became cloudy and we rested, and in the evening walked in the town. The town is much more dirty and townish than I expected it to be. There is something that reminds one of Scotland in it. 'The Canongate by the Sea side' was the first description of it that occurred to me. The houses are not so picturesque as I expected to find them and the general dirtiness and smokiness give a forbidding instead of attractive look such as picturesque sea side places generally have.[10] The children, many of them barefoot, are awfully dirty. As for the dangers of the place which we have heard so much - they are certainly real if care be not taken. The cliffs have a treacherous edge and are consequently dangerous above and below. The beach under the East cliff is especially dangerous as the sea comes close up to the cliff at high water and rises rapidly. The river is very deep at high water and there are plenty of places where chldren could slip into it. The pier has no railings. Sometimes I wonder any Whitby children get beyond childhood, but I suppose those that escape these pitfalls are skilful and bold in proportion to the dangers by which they are surrounded.

[June 23rd Saturday] In the morning while the rest of the party went to the beach I walked to the top of the highest hill on this side of the river. I find it is called Swarthoue, or Swarthouecross, probably from the former cross ways upon it. On the top of the hill is a mound which is visible from Whitby.[11] From the East Cliff, the whole country on the west of the river is seen rising to this mound, consequently, I was attracted to it. The distance is about four miles and here you touch the moor and this too is the nearest point to Whitby at which you can touch it. The road lies through a rather bare country. I turned off for

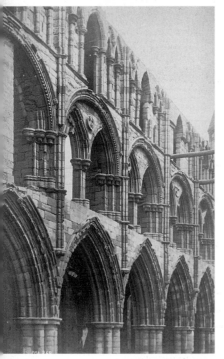

a little way through the fields and the village of Newholm, but whether I gained or lost in distance I do not know. The first sign of moorland was a bit of furzy ground but heather appeared about the mound. The view was very extensive but the air too hazy to show it well. Ridges of hill were to be seen on both sides of the Esk which are all bare moorland. Pale misty ridges stretching for many miles. There is a small quarry of a kind of sandstone just on the side of the hill.

In the afternoon we all went to the Abbey. The ruins are fine and the Abbey was once a very beautiful building (Figure 5). The stone is much scooped out by the weather. We also looked into the market which is a covered one but we were too late in the day. (Fred was charmed to see some pigs run into a house from their pen under the town hall). In the evening did some shopping.

[June 24th Sunday] In the morning to St Ninian's, an old chapel of ease to the parish church, which has lately been done up to some very high notions.[12] In the afternoon Polly and I went to the Parish Church. This is one of the quaintest buildings I ever saw. Originally a

Figure 5. The ruins of Whitby Abbey, a photograph by F M Sutcliffe. *From the collection of A. Whitworth*

Norman building, and consequently older than the Abbey which is Early English, it has had nearly all the architecture taken out of it by the beautifyings and restorations of, I suppose, various times since the Reformation. There are pews and galleries, a wooden ceiling painted a light colour, with sky-lights breaking out from it, and a towering pulpit rising above reading desk etc. in the middle of the church. A bit of fine Norman arch is just seen at the entrance to the chancel but this arch is crossed by a smart gallery in which is the pew of the great people of the Hall - the back of the pew being to the East and its front facing West into the church. The chancel is like a carpeted room beyond this arch and gallery. In spite of all this there is something wonderfully cheerful about the place which reminds one of a ship more than of anything else.[13]

At a second visit I found one other bit of Norman work in the arch of a side window but this and the chancel arch are all that I could see. After the service while we were looking about the Curate who had read the prayers pointed out a curious monument put up in memory of a number of men lost by the capsizing of the Whitby lifeboat (Figure 6). So much money was raised in consequence of a letter to *The Times* by the Rector that it became necessary to advertise that no more was wanted. The balance left after doing what was necessary in charity was used for this monument on which was cut an extract from the Rector's letter to *The Times*.[14] The Curate added that it is said in Whitby that some wished '[?Navy] George' had been in the boat, but for the truth of this he could not vouch as it was before he came to Whitby.

Figure 6. St Mary's Church, Whitby, the Lifeboat Memorial. *Photograph by A. Whitworth*

In the evening we went to St Michael's, a church on the other side of the river.[15] Then had a stroll.

[June 25th Monday] Sunny morning. Hired a machine to take us to the Mulgrave Castle woods. The road used to give good sea views but since the new [railway] line has been made some of the best views have been shut out by a wooden fence. There are some fine iron viaducts on this new line passing over what in the Isle of Wight would be called chines. The line is not yet open but when it is [it] will open up the coast to the mouth of the Tees.[16] At Sandsend you turn inland up a ravine which is very pretty at its entrance and has a village by the sea. The Mulgrave woods here begin and the drive through them is extremely beautiful. The sides of the ravine are covered with woods. We got out at the usual place to meet the carriage at a summer house called the Hermitage, then wound round to the old castle - a ruin standing on a high ridge among the woods with deep ravines below it. Thunder began to growl in the distance when we reached the castle

Figure 7. The two castles at Mulgrave and the woods.

so that we did not stay long but drove on through the remainder of the woods and grounds.[17] We passed over Lover's Leap, a steep precipitous descent in (I suppose) the shale. Caught a glimpse of the modern castle and crossing a bit of open park left the grounds and returned to Whitby by road (Figure 7).

The beauty of the day was over when we had returned but in the afternoon I walked to Ruswarp by the fields and crossing the bridge went up to Cock Mill, a small cluster of houses (the mill has been pulled down) on the banks of a little stream which comes down to the Esk. I was very much surprised to find a very pretty waterfall; I dare say very much improved by the loss of the mill which would draw off so much water from the fall that there would hardly be anything left. The rock here is very picturesque and the bed of the little stream is full of great lumps of stone. In the evening I looked in at the Museum (Figure 8). I should think it is very good for local geological specimens. There are some fine fossil reptiles which are found here and I saw the great crocodile eighteen feet long and with a head twelve inches broad which is perhaps the greatest curiosity in the Museum.[18]

[June 26th Tuesday] Fotty being five years old today, she and Fred and a little girl her own age, Mrs Clifford's daughter, had a donkey ride in the morning, to the great delight of them all. I then went to the East Pier which is reached by a long sloping bridge or wooden stair reaching from the cliff, as it does not actually join the cliff, an opening being left for the sea to sweep through.[19] These piers are made for business not for company. They are very massive buildings of cut sandstone with a lighthouse at the end of each to mark the entrance at high water during the night. The afternoon was rainy. In the evening I went on the East Cliff. It was raining still. There was a fine sea.

Figure 8. The former Museum and Public Bathing Establishment in Pier Road, today a fish restaurant.

[June 27th Wednesday] In the morning I took the train to Goathland to see some waterfalls. At the end of the village is the little church, a simple building without a tower in the sort of no-style of its date, 1821, but pleasant to see (with its one little bell) standing on the very edge of the moors.[20] There was a smell of peat smoke in the air and one might be said not only to touch the moor here, as at Swarthoue, but to feel it also.

Getting a key from a farmhouse I descended by a rough path to the banks of the 'beck' and passing through a gate which has been put up in consequence of the visitors to the fall taking away so many ferns. I walked a short distance up the stream to Mallyan Spout which falls into it from a little side stream. The views from the high ground had been beautiful, the height of the village being considerable and the hill country on a large scale. The river scenery below was equally good in its way. The great lumps of rock among which the stream flows being quite worthy of a mountain stream. The 'spout' suddenly appeared on the left - the water all broken into a drizzly spray leaping from a projecting point of rock. The fall is said to be about one hundred feet high. The farmer's wife who gave me the key said that sometimes it shoots out far into the beck and carries vast quantities of stones over with it.

My next point was another fall on the beck itself, called Nelly Aire Foss (the first two words pronounced short as one, Nellyer). This fall is in the open moor though upon the edge of some fields and the road to it gave one a notion of the moorland. The whole ground is covered with heather and brakes which last are now young and bright green. Here and there grey stones break out of the heather and runnels of water make spongy places. The waterfall is reached by anything but a 'company' path and is well worth seeing, not high but broad, the band of rock down which the stream leaps crossing the river. [It is a pecularity of the place that there is so little enclosing and charging for the sights, the waterfalls with the exception of Mallyan Spout seem to be open for anyone who cares to go after them.][21]

Returning to the village I had some bread and cheese at the inn and then went to see another fall on another beck. This last is called Thomasin Foss and as a fall is the most of the three. Having descended the stream to its next union with another beck I returned towards Goathland up its course, the path being among the great stones and lumps of rock which fill its bed. Reaching the lowest level I was obliged to wade across taking off shoes and socks and then quickly reached the upper and principal fall which is a clear leap reminding me of the 'Ladies Fall' as it is called at Pont Werth Vaughan. The whole scene, the wall of rock which causes the fall and the circular hollow or basin into which the stream leaps filled with great lumps of rock and overhung with trees was very beautiful. Having made my way up the bank I found myself on the railway and getting a labourer on the line to pass me across the bridge I made my way to the station not thinking it worth my while to go after the other falls in the neighbourhood. I got back to Whitby in time for dinner which was later than usual to give me the opportunity of catching it.

As one gets used to the train journeys through these vallies it becomes easier to pick out the best points in the scenery and one can see more of it and enjoy it more. There is a beautiful bit under the great hill between Grosmont and Sleights where a precipitous shaly slope comes down to the Esk, overhung by woods and the heathery and ferny hillside above all. The views from Goathland were really fine, the glens so deep and their sides so beautiful with fields and woods and the very scent of the hillsides and of the woods is delightful.*

*Turf is burnt here as well as peat and turf stacks are to [be] seen on the hill tops and at the farm houses. The sheep of the moor are small, white and horned with long hairy wool. I like hill sheep and their fleeces.

In the afternoon shopped and rain came on.

[June 28th Thursday] Morning and afternoon on the beach. In the evening on the West Cliff. Heavy air and a great show for rain. It being Coronation Day the church bells rang and a flag was flying from the short stumpy tower.

[June 29th Friday] In the morning which was bright and sunny Polly heard at a shop that the Scarbro the steamer from Scarborough would return there at two o'clock instead of three [o'clock] as usual, so we suddenly decided to go by it (Figure 9).[22] We dined early therefore and started at two o'clock. Fotty fortunately was content to be left behind having Katie to play with. The 'Scarbro' was lying in the river the tide being high enough so that we had merely to slip on board. We had to steam some way out and round a buoy which is moored off the river's mouth. On this buoy is a bell with four clappers outside it. The bell is fixed so that as the buoy moves on the water one or other of the clappers strikes it on the outside. I have several times since heard it on the shore - a melancholy sound. The sea was just as it should be to make a trip pleasant in a steamer. Enough motion to be like the sea and not enough to make one uneasy.

The day was beautiful and the coast passed before us in fine grey colouring. A little beyond the high lights Scarborough Castle was visible, the keep looking large on its rock. One gets a totally different idea of Robin Hood's Bay from the water. The green slopes which form such a beautiful semicircle when seen from the land are here reduced in size and importance and the great hill ending in the Peak headland is the chief attraction. This is really grand and the headland becomes more imposing as you pass immediately before it. I believe it is about 600 feet high and certainly is a very fine cliff, rising in three steps which were marked by lines of the sunshine on the green terraces, the colour delicately subdued by distance, the face of the cliff

Figure 9. The *Streonshalh*, reputedly Whitby's first passenger pleasure steamship.

Figure 10. A Jockey Carriage at Scarborough, 1895.

being grey rock in shade. This is the point at which the hills of the moorland touch the sea most closely, that is to say they break down here from higher ground closer than elsewhere.

The next point of interest was Haiburn Wyke [Hayburn Wyke] where there is again (as at Robin Hood's Bay and at Whitby) a break or fault in the strata. This forms a sort of broken gully to the beach. With a diagram in a little book I have bought here, *A Guide to the Geology of the Yorkshire Coast,* these matters were easily seen though in nature the hard edges of the strata are worn away and softened down and the whole veiled by vegetation.[23] At Haiburn Wyke the cliffs are still high but after this they sink, and from Cloughton Wyke to Scarborough are much lower.

As we drew nearer Scarborough gun practice was going on from the top of the Castle cliff. White puffs of smoke darted out and floated before the cliff.[24] The effect was very fine. The cliff itself is a grand one running so boldly as it does out into the sea and sinking sheer down to the water. We passed near it having seen the northern part of Scarborough and its pier, and then rounding the rock entered the bay on its southern side. Here the tower of the 'Grand' Hotel came into view, this last a huge mass apparantly built in rivalry with the Castle cliff. We landed on the harbour pier after a passage of two hours and getting at once into a carriage drove to the Spa.

The old town and the harbour looked most picturesque and unlike Whitby, inviting. The tide was out and the sands were dotted with people on foot and horseback and in low phaetons with boy postillions (Figure 10). The sands look like velvet. At the Spa we had coffee and walked about the grounds winding up by the lift which we saw at work (one carriage going up while another was coming down) to the bridge, by which we left it.[25]

The view from these grounds is beautiful, more so than I had remembered it to be. Of course there is no forgetting the general view of Scarborough (Figure 11) and it is a place to a certain extent seen in one view, but the long line of cliffs forming the southern side of the bay looked more beautiful than I had remembered thinking. Broken with green slopes on their upper parts. Something was due to the splendid day. The Spa buildings and grounds are in some sort the Crystal Palace by the seaside, and the *Grand Hotel* is the elephant of the wild beast show.

I ought to have said that during our approach to Scarborough and miles away from it, Oliver's Mount was the conspicuous object, looking like a Table Mountain in miniature. This hill which has such a curiously artificial look when seen from the North and especially when seen near is really but the end of a ridge as we found on leaving Scarborough, for the train runs some way by the side of this ridge southwards.

I ought to have [also] mentioned something similar [which] we saw when we drove to Robin Hood's Bay; a long mound-like hill pricking up to the South which our driver said was Langdale End. On leaving the Spa we went to the principal street which is a very good one full of shops and broad and long. There is a bar or gate which though it does not look old, must surely be a restored old one.[26]

We had no time to go to the Castle or Oliver's Mount but soon took the train and returned to Whitby by way of Malton and Pickering.[27] We had not left Scarborough long before grand thunder clouds came up and broke over us. The Wolds were on our left and we had a good view of them. In character like all chalk hills I know but cultivated to the top. Here and there their nature could be seen in a white road and white pits. They rise abruptly and are decidedly hilly. We passed through the storm which however came up a second time at Malton Junction where we had to wait some time. We then had no more of it but saw its effects on the swollen streams of the moors.

Between Levisham and Goathland stations the line crosses the water parting of the hills and goes for some miles in the midst of the moorland though this was not so apparent as our first journey because we were not used to the country and the fact of being in a valley took off from the appearance of the moor. The stream which flowed down to the North seemed to be the fullest. At Goathland station it made a

Figure 11. Scarborough foreshore and harbour lighthouse in the nineteenth century.

furious leap down a rocky step which I tried to get Fred to see. Poor
Fred was now, however, so tired that he could look with pleasure at
nothing and when at Grosmont I pointed out the iron works all
glowing in the light of their own fires, a most picturesque sight, and
one which took me quite by surprise, it only drew tears from his eyes.[28]
On reaching Whitby we were told that the storm had been very sharp
indeed and was only just over. This was at quarter past ten [at night].

[June 30th Saturday] In the morning we went to see some jet-
works on a larger scale than those we saw before.[29] In other respects
matters were managed much the same except that here was a gas
engine; that is to say an engine worked by gas instead of steam, but
how I do not exactly understand. The men were many of them in blue

Figure 12. The Market Place, Whitby with the old Toll Booth erected in 1788.

blouses which gave a French look to the workshop. We also went to the market (Figure 12) and being much earlier than before saw it well filled with sellers if not buyers. In the upper room used for a vegetable market women and sometimes men from the country were sitting round by the wall with baskets of eggs and butter before them waiting for purchasers but not pushing the sale. Finished with the beach.

In the afternoon I took the train to Sleights intending to see a waterfall called Falling Foss but finding the distance too great for so late in the day and as there was still a threatening of storm I contented myself with walking to Grosmont and returning by train from that station.

Between Whitby and Sleights the train passed the viaduct which is being built across the Esk for the new Scarbro' line (Figure 13).[30] I saw that some of the circular brick foundations for a future pier had been displaced by the flooding river. The beck on which is the waterfall I went to see was still flooded though the water had subsided a good deal, its traces over its banks being very apparent. The road to Grosmont lies high up on the hill side and this part of the valley is called Eskdaleside, a pleasant name; and there are beautiful views from it, the ridge of Swarthoue (as it here shows itself) being opposite. Although there is so much variety of scenery about Whitby the

Figure 13. The railway viaduct, Larpool, under construction.

reason is not that things are on a small scale for the reverse is the case, but from the position of the place at the mouth of a hill stream.

[July 1st Sunday] In the morning Fred and I went to the old church, the rest of the party to St Ninian's. In the evening we went to St Ninian's again.[31]

[July 2nd Monday] [The family visit Rievaulx Abbey]

[July 3rd Tuesday] Rainy with thunder off and on all day.

[July 4th Wednesday] Miss Bailey returned to Norwich starting by the 9.15 train. We took a walk in the morning round by the Abbey. In the afternoon we contented ourselves with the town.

[July 5th Thursday] Morning the beach. I went to the East beach which is composed of a layer of shale in which are to be found fossils and in which I actually saw Ammonites though I couldn't get them out.[32] The cliffs are fine seen from below. I walked as far as a long low black headland of shale which runs out at a place called Saltwick and here mounted the cliff and so returned by the top of it. Here were formerly alum works and above the low black headland is a sort of recess in the cliffs which reminds me of those at Black Gang Chine [Isle of Wight]. At the bottom of the hollow is a small building, a shed (closed always when I have seen it) with bright green shutters, and some tables and seats are dotted about. I have never seen anyone here and don't know what may be the meaning of it, but I call it, mentally, Neptune's Tea Garden.[33] On returning I was surprised to find how much the tide had already gained up the beach.

In the afternoon we went to Mr Clifford's workshop across the river. He is a joiner.[34] His father was there and I having enquired about a corn cutter he most obligingly offered to cut my corns, which accordingly he did in the evening, and gave me a great deal of comfort for the rest of my stay. I must say that I never saw a more obliging people than we have met in Yorkshire.

[July 6th Friday] [The writer takes an excursion to Roseberry Topping and Guisborough]

[July 7th Saturday] In the morning we went on the East beach and fell in with a man collecting fossils, who picked out of the shale several Ammonites (St Hilda's snakes) for us - also some Belemnites and ferns and from the cliff a bit of coal. Rested in the afternoon and in the evening strolled on the pier.

[July 8th Sunday] Feeling seedy I rested till evening, then we walked in the fields leading to Ruswarp by a paved path.[35]

[July 9th Monday] Morning beach, afternoon rest - Evening - Town.

[July 10th Tuesday] [The writer makes an excursion to Ripon and Fountains Abbey]

[July 11th Wednesday] In the morning the beach. In the afternoon Fred had a donkey ride on the beach and in the evening we went on the pier. There was a sale of American watches by auction at a sort of Cheap John's carriage close to the pier.[36]

[July 12th Thursday] Morning the town. Showery. In the afternoon wrote journal. In the evening on the East Cliff. Very stormy day.

[July 13th Friday] Today we took our last excursion from Whitby in order to see Runswick and Staithes. Hired a carriage and started about 10.30am (Figure 14). At Sandsend the road mounts up to Lythe. The hill is long and steep and is called Lythe Bank. Bank seems to be the word used here for a hill. Thus there is Blue Bank over Sleights leading up to the moor. Lythe Church (Figure 15) from Whitby seems to be on the top of the hill but is really not so. The only peculiarity about it I noticed was that each little pinnacle of the tower had a vane on it instead of one in the centre.[37] The country becomes bare and you still mount up to a considerable height. There is then a very extensive view towards Swarthoue and over many miles of moorland ranges of hill. You then descend into a hollow, cultivated, but rather bare of trees, the ridge forming a crescent touching the sea at each end.

Putting up the horse at the *Sheffield Hotel* we walked down to Runswick, which is a fishing village built on the lowest stage of the cliff at an inner corner of a deep bay. The ground sweeps down to the beach at the bottom of the bay, broken and picturesque. The village is dotted about on the slope with a sandstone crag above it and is curious, picturesque and smelly. We returned to the hotel for bread and cheese which we got at last but thought that we never should have got, and then drove on through Hinderwell to Staithes. This is also a fishing village and more curious than the other, as it is built in a ravine which

LIVERY STABLES,
West Cliff & Skinner St.,
WHITBY.

FOSTER & SON,
LIVERY STABLE KEEPERS,
16, SKINNER STREET, WHITBY,

In thanking their friends for their patronage during the past, beg to announce they have added to their Skinner Street Mews the New and Extensive Stables and Coach Houses, situate on the West Cliff, adjoining the Royal Hotel Stables, and nearly opposite the West Cliff Club House. The Stables have been fitted up in the most complete style, having special regard to the comfort of their horses and the convenience of their patrons.

Cabs, Carriages, Waggonettes, Dog Carts, Landaus and Funeral Equipages all complete, supplied on the Shortest Notice and on the most reasonable terms.

Horses taken in at Livery. Lock-up Coach Houses.

Figure 14. An advertisement for a Livery Stable, one of many to be found in Whitby.

Figure 15. Lythe church before restoration. *Tom Watson*

winds down to the sea. There is one long street which follows its wind-
ings to the beach. The place therefore does not appear until you are
close up to it, and such houses as are not in the street itself are built
on the slope - rough stone steps sometimes lead up to them. The
stream is once crossed by a wooden bridge (Figure 16) which when
we saw it was most picturesqely draped with fishing nets. The sides of
the ravine are steep and rocky, the layers of rock on the left or northern
side having broken down towards the beach. The other hill rises also
very abruptly towards the sea and ends in fine perpendicular grey
cliffs.

Here, as at Runswick, the smells are past a joke, dead fish lying

Figure 16. The wooden bridge at *Statithes*.

about in all directions. But the place has a most cheerful living look or had when we were there, and is certainly one of the most curious places I have seen. Captain Cook was here apprenticed for a short time to a grocer but the house in which he served his time has, I believe, disappeared.

Above the entrance to the village the ravine is crossed by a new iron viaduct of the railway from Whitby to Saltburn, the highest part of which one driver told me is 152 feet high above the stream. This line is now finished but not yet opened.[38] It was curious to see the station we passed apparently in perfect order but silent and deserted. Beyond Staithes is Boulby Cliff formed by the beginning of a range of hills, the most northerly of the group in the North East of Yorkshire. The cliff is between six and seven hundred feet high. We could just see where it began to break down towards the sea. We were here certainly into Cleveland again. On our return (we walked down to the sea and left the carriage waiting for us at the entrance to Staithes) we got out to look into the churchyard of Hinderwell where there is a well which is called St Hilda's and which supplies the whole village with water. It has lately been covered up and a pump put up which Fred was very pleased to work for a woman who came for a pail of water.

After tea I walked round by the piers to Ruswarp, crossing the river and returning by Cock Mill. Then Polly and I had a turn on the pier.

[July 14th Saturday] In the morning Fred and I walked along the West Cliff to a place we passed yesterday to get some wild orchid roots. The sea was beautiful in colour and there were fine breakers. In the afternoon to the market. More was doing in the open market place than before. In the evening on the pier.

[July 15th Sunday] In the morning to St John's church.[39] Wet afternoon and very cold. Fred nine [years old] today. In the evening I went to the Iron Church and afterwards took a turn on the pier.[40] There were, I believe, a few flakes of sleet or snow in the rain this afternoon. A great [word illegible] was quite comfortable in the evening. Fine seas and big waves rolling into the mouth of the river.

[July 16th Monday] Our last day at Whitby. On Tuesday an accident happened near the High Lights; a Whitby boy of about fourteen fell from the cliff and after lying some hours was found still alive and brought to Whitby. He was taking his uncle's dinner to him. I have never mentioned the Roman Catholic church here which is a fine one. We looked in one day in passing. There are a great many Roman Catholics in this neighbourhood. Egton Bridge is composed principally of them and a little moorland village called Ugthorpe has a Roman Catholic church in it. I suppose at the Reformation this part

Figure 17. Saltwick Tea Gardens.

of the country was so inaccessible that the doctrines did not spread so freely here. At any rate the fact remains that this is a great place for Roman Catholics whatever may be the explanation of it.

I have intended to mention a Whitby peculiarity which pleases me - the donkeys which bring in milk in large tins and which are regularly seen about the streets particularly gathered together at a public house in Flowergate.[41] The fish women too are somewhat in the Edinburgh style and the cries reminded us of Edinburgh. The river is very small at low water and at high water we have often seen it most distinctly marked outside the harbour like a great yellow tongue lolling out of the harbour mouth, the grey sea water sharply defined against it.

There is ship building going on here, but all the ships are now built of iron.[42] It was here that Captain Cook's ship was built in which he made his second voyage. There is a model of it at the museum. The fish market by the dockside is merely a space on the pavement at an angle against some projecting houses. Here the fish is laid out on the stones and bought by the women who carry it about the town.[43] Into the river, of course, all sorts of refuse is cast. One day in the early part of our visit I saw a red stream shooting from a pipe in the wall and forming a red pool in the river below. This was from a butcher's near the bridge. However, the tide sweeps all away.

In the morning we contented ourselves with the town. In the afternoon I went on the East Pier and on the cliffs as far as Saltwick. The tide was in and the waves broke on the cliffs. At Saltwick I went on the beach in the bay just beyond what I call Neptune's Tea Garden (Figure 17). This bay is the finest bit of coast scenery so near Whitby. The cliffs are grey rock broken with green grassy slopes. The lower part of the cliff is shale, which here and there forms smooth surfaces not unlike those shown in a haystack where a clean cut has been made. In these smooth surfaces, which, by the by, are greasy to touch, the shale shows itself to be stone. It often, however, looks like mere earth where it forms slopes, either rounded or hollowed, from the way in which the weather acts upon the thin layers of which the rock is composed, covering the entire surface with a litter of small flakes. The colouring of the smooth surfaces was here very varied and beautiful. In general this shale has a black look and two low black headlands of it run out, one from each point of the bay. A little trickling rill comes down through the tea garden, first dripping from the upper cliff which seems to be sandstone. Where this rill reaches the beach it has cut its way deep through the barrier of black shale.

The beach in the bay is of rich warm reddish sand. The grey rounded lower step of the East Cliff at Whitby is composed of shale and this is I suppose alum shale for there are many alum works formerly at Saltwick and elsewhere in the Lias formations. Here and there large stones appear embedded in it.[44]

In the evening we went into the cliff walks of the Saloon which we had seen from without only until now (Figure 18). There is a fine concert room and theatre in the centre of the saloon building with a reading room at one end and refreshment rooms at the other. Outside an asphalt terrace with another below it, consequently under cover. A sort of summer house for the band and walks winding down the cliff.[45] Tennis grounds are on the top. The whole thing a faint - very faint - reflection of Scarborough, but dreary in the extreme, at any rate on such an evening as this which was more like October than July.

Little Katie's birthday being the day after tomorrow and Fred's yesterday, we had had this evening a grand tea drinking in honour of these two great events.

[July 17th Tuesday] We left Whitby at 9.15am for Lincoln . . .

THE PAVILION.

Figure 18. West Cliff Saloon, known as the Pavilion.

Notes and References

1. Norfolk Record Office, MS Eaton 4.2.71 VII.

2. Gard, R. (Ed.) *The Observant Traveller*, 1989, 116, nos.402-419.

3. Mrs Clifford does not seem to have stayed at 6 South Terrace for very long. She was not there in either the 1879 or 1890 Trade Directories. South Terrace is part of the earliest development of the West Cliff, dating from 1848.

4. Whitby was now at about the peak of its success in the jet trade, very much fostered by the Victorian culture of mourning, encouraged by the Queen herself. The 1890 Directory lists 166 manufacturers of jet alone, as well as 10 rough jet merchants. Each of these men would have had a number of employees and it is claimed that up to 1500 persons were employed by the jet trade at its peak.

5. These flagged paths, often known locally as 'monk's trods', are the old packhorse tracks used before the development of the turnpike roads. It is usually impossible to date them, but there is no doubt that they represent ancient routes.

6. The 'machine' would no doubt be a pony trap, hired from one of the local hotels or livery stables.

7. Legend has it that Robin Hood and Little John fired arrows from the Abbey tower and stone pillars marked the spots where their arrows fell. The tradition is quite an early one, perhaps influenced by the name of nearby Robin Hood's Bay. Dobson, R.B. & Taylor, J. *Rhymes of Robyn Hood: An Introduction to the English Outlaw*, 1989, p180,307.

8. The story of Beggar's Bridge is told in Horne's *Guide to Whitby*, 4th edition, 1895, p.45-59.

9. Grosmont was the source of ironstone from the Pecten and Avicula beds and because of its remoteness, blast furnaces were set up here in 1863 so that pig iron rather than the more bulky ironstone could be taken out via the railway. The furnaces were close to the railway station and ceased to operate in 1891. Clarke, B.W. & Soulsby, J.A. *The Story of Grosmont: Church and Village*, 1979; Spratt, D.A. & Harrison, B.J.D. *The North York Moors Landscape Heritage*, 1989, p183.

10. Eaton gained an unfortunate first impression of Whitby which he later modified. The smokiness,

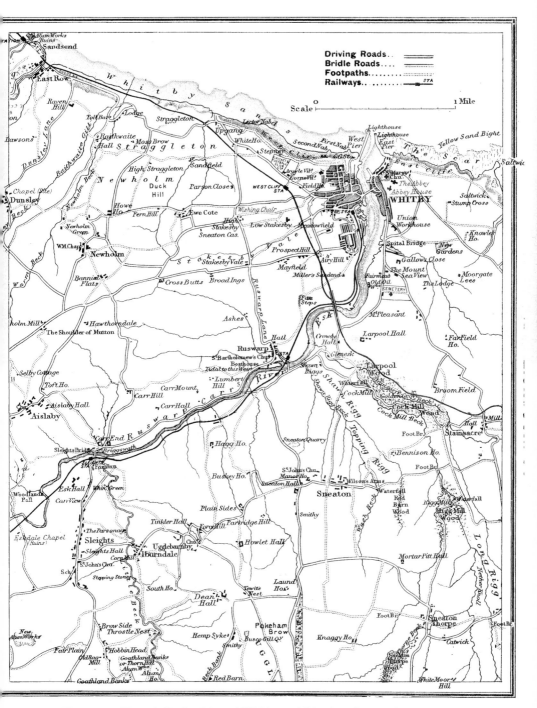

Figure 19. Horne's Pocket Map of Whitby and District, nineteenth century.

dirt and poverty, however, were real enough, judging from Sutcliffe's photographs. Whitby was not primarily a seaside town and all those towns which tried to combine a resort functon with a harbour trade or a fishing fleet tended to find the two elements fought with each other.

11. Swarthowe is a Bronze Age burial mound, like so many other of the 'howes' on the North York Moors. When it was excavated by Samuel Anderson in the 1850s he found an urn and two jet rings. Elgee, J. *Early Man in North East Yorkshire,* 1930, p.110.

12. St Ninian's was built in 1778 as a proprietary chapel, owned by thirty original subscribers, whose descendants still own it. In 1881-2, under the influence of a very high Anglo-Catholic priest, St Ninian's underwent a liturgical transformation which affected the nave and chancel, although the gallery which runs around three sides is still virtually in its Georgian state.

13. Eaton was unusual for his time in liking the Parish Church, which one Victorian parson described as 'now perhaps the most depraved sacred building in the kingdom'. It was the undisguisedly domestic style of the Georgian church which the Victorians could not tolerate, needing a church to be set apart by its architecture from the everyday world. Visitors have constantly remarked upon its ship-like feel, which is created by the skylights and the galleries, with their cramped headroom.

14. The story of the 1861 lifeboat disaster and the relief fund is told at length in Humble, A.F. *The Rowing Life Boats of Whitby,* 1974, p64ff.

15. St Michael's church, a small Gothic building with a bell-cote, stood on the east side of the river near Tin Ghaut. It was erected in 1847-8 and was demolished some years ago. A plaque in the present car park wall commemorates the site.

16. This railway line was the short-lived Whitby, Redcar & Middlesbrough Union Railway. Begun in 1871 it was not opened until December 1883 because of engineering difficulties and bad work-manship by the first contractor, which had to be rectified. It closed in 1958 and most of the iron viaducts were demolished soon after. Despite all its problems it was a very scenic railway which opened up the cliffs of Cleveland to passengers. Hoole, K. *The Whitby, Redcar and Middlesbrough Union Railway,* 1981.

17. Mulgrave Woods formed a popular excursion from Whitby last century. The very extensive grounds contain the present house, home of the Marquis of Normanby, known as Mulgrave Castle, an older core with extensions dating from 1786 and 1805-14, and its two predecessors, the ruins of the medieval castle and the remains of the Norman motte and bailey. The woods are not generally open to the public today.

18. This is the superb example of the *Teleosaurus Chapmani,* still to be seen in the Whitby Museum. It was found in the alum shale at Saltwick and purchased for £7 in 1824. Browne, H.B. *The Story of Whitby Museum,* 1949, p9-10.

19. This bridge or ladder has since time immemorial been known as the 'Spa Ladder', although its original site is unknown. The two Spas in the town were on the West Cliff and in Bagdale; none is known on the East Cliff. Due to the erosion of the cliff there have been many successors to the struc-ture which Eton saw.

20. The old church has since been replaced (in the 1890s) with a rather more conventional struc-ture with a squat tower. Until the railway arrived, Goathland was a remote and quiet moorland village; the railway opened up its scenic attractions, especially the waterfalls, to a mass of summer visitors.

21. This last sentence appears to have been added as an after-thought by Eaton.

22. The *Scarborough* was a paddle-steamer of 142 tons, built in London in 1866. She was the largest and best appointed steamer to use Scarborough as a base and survived until 1914. Godfrey, A. *Pleasure Steamers of Old Yorkshire,* nd, p19,33, plate 11.

23. This was probably Simpson, M. *A Guide to the Geology of the Yorkshire Coast,* 1856. Martin Simpson was involved with the Whitby Museum as lecturer and keeper and then as curator from 1837 until 1892. He was a pioneer in the science of geology but because he did not illustrate the fossils he described his work was largely ignored by later experts.

24. The site of Scarborough Castle has been used for coastal defence since Roman times. Remains of a Roman signal station can be seen within the medieval fortifications. In and after the English Civil War gun batteries were placed on the slope of the cliff to protect the harbour. In 1850 the Admiralty placed a 32pdr gun in this battery for use by the coastguard, which may have been the one Eaton saw. [However, at a later date in the 19th century the Admiralty held trials of the new 'Whitworth' field gun off the cliff-top (Ed.)]. *Bulmer's History, Topography and Directory of North Yorkshire,* 1890, p1023.

25. Scarborough still retains its hydraulic inclined tramways. The earliest was the South Cliff Tramway, near the Spa, built in 1875. Another, the Queen's Parade Tramway, followed in 1878. It was short-lived, but the Central Tramway near the Grand Hotel, opened in 1881, is still in use. It is the first of these that Eaton describes. Edwards, M. (Ed.) *Scarborough 966-1966,* 1966, p78.

26. This was the Westborough Bar, built (as Eaton suspected) as recently as 1847, in a medieval style. It was demolished in 1890, soon after his visit.

27. They had to return the long way round via Malton because the direct railway link along the cliffs to Whitby was not opened until July 1885. It closed in 1965. Like the Middlesbrough line it involved considerable engineering works and was sometimes unworkable in winter conditions. Lidster, J.R. *The Scarborough & Whitby Railway,* 1977.

28. see above

29. This jet workshop, the subject of a well-known photograph by Sutcliffe, can be identified as William Wright's premises in Haggersgate, the lathes of which were powered by a gas engine. Shaw, M. *Frank Meadow Sutcliffe; a Third Selection,* 1990, p26, neg.27-38.

30. Lidster, 1977, Plates 49-52 illustrate the building of this viaduct at Larpool in 1882-4, from photographs taken by Sutcliffe.

31. *see above*

32. Eaton was not the first or last to be unable to extract ammonites from the shale. Many of these are actually thin and fragile casts or else heavily pyritised. The best examples are to be found in the large round nodules which occur in bands throughout the alum shale. These nodules were once calcined to make 'Roman cement' at Sandsend. [In Whitby ammonites are often used for decoration in buildings most notably 10A Cliff Street (Ed.)].

33. In Horne's *Guide to Whitby,* 1895, there is an advertisement for this tea garden. The small stone building, covered with thatch, may have been a survivor of the alum works here.

34. Robert Clifford, joiner, is recorded at Sanders Yard, Church Street, in 1879. *Post Office Directory of Yorkshire, North and East Riding.*

35. The walk across Ruswarp Fields by the flagged path is still a very attractive one. A flight of steps, known as 'Fitts Steps', leading down from the old river terrace to the water meadows of the Esk, is reputed to be haunted.

36. From just before the middle of the 19th century mass-produced American watches were beginning to drive out the local handmade product by mere cheapness. Many were sold in auctions and 'fancy bazaars' rather than by jewellers and watch-makers.

37. In 1910 this church was taken down and replaced by a much grander one. The whole process was captured on photographs by Tom Watson, of Lythe. Richardson, G. *Tom Watson Photographer of Lythe, near Whitby,* Est. 1892, 1992, p85-91, 123-5.

38. see above.

39. St John's church stands in the angle of Baxtergate and Brunswick Street. It was built in 1848. At the time of writing the church is the subject of a redundancy scheme and its future hangs in the balance.

40. The 'iron church' was the first St Hilda's on the West Cliff. It was hastily erected to cater for the summer visitors and the burgeoning population of the West Cliff and was replaced by the present grand stone structure between 1884-6, although the tower was not completed until this century. The new church was illustrated in *The Building News,* 23 October 1885, reproduced in White, A. *A History of Whitby,* 1993, p53.

41. This was the *Abbey Inn,* Flowergate, where the milkmen and their donkeys were caught on camera by Sutcliffe (neg.B 45). The inn has since been demolished but a yard exists off Flowergate named Abbey Inn Yard.

42. By the 1880s the only shipyard still in operation, building iron ships, was that of Turnbull's at Whitehall. The yard is long since closed but the slipway is still visible below the new high-level road bridge.

43. Sutcliffe photographed these fisherwomen many times and they also appear in du Maurier's cartoons of the period, carrying fish in large wicker baskets on their heads.

44. These are the nodules referred to above (32).

45. The Spa (or Saloon, as it was sometimes known), was created as part of the West Cliff development by Sir George Elliot, MP for Whitby, in 1880.

5. Early Aviators of The East Coast

by Alan Whitworth

INCREDIBLE AS IT SEEMS it is less than one hundred years since man first flew in a heavier-than-air machine when the American Wright brothers, Orville and Wilbur, made the first flight of forty yards on 17 December 1903 at Kitty Hawk, North Carolina. Yet since that date tremendous and rapid strides have been made from those first faltering steps to that giant leap for mankind when another group of Americans flew to the moon and back.

Notwithstanding that Americans have been the first in these significant events in aviation history, here in this country, it is perhaps not fully appreciated that Yorkshire has been in the forefront in pioneering aeroplanes and manned flight, and in particular, that the East Coast area could be said to be the cradle of aviation development in England.

Figure 1. Sir George Cayley, aged seventy.

For instance, it is possibly forgotten that it was Sir George Cayley (1771-1857) (Figure 1), an English engineer, who lived in the village of Brompton, near Scarborough, who pioneered developments in aviation in the nineteenth century, and who constructed the first successful man-carrying glider in 1853 (Figure 2 and 3).

The conquest of the air appears to have caught the imagination of men around here almost from the time aircraft were first built. In October 1908, the American Samuel Cody made the first powered flight in Britain over a distance of nearly five hundred yards.

Figure 2. One of Cayley's drawings taken from his notebook for a flying machine capable of carrying a man.

At Filey, by the summer of 1910, the aeroplane was a familiar sight in the skies thereabout, when the beach at Filey Bay became Yorkshire's main take-off and landing strip, and was a base of the Yorkshire Light Aeroplane Club, founded in 1909.

One of the first aircraft to arrive at Filey, was a 25 horse-power Bleriot plane piloted by John W House, of Bradford, who in July 1910 combined his flying exploits with his honeymoon! Lucky for his bride, the groom survived injuries soon after their arrival, when his monoplane crashed and did a cartwheel on landing following a short flying session.

During the next two years the people of Filey followed with great

Figure 3. The finished design for Cayley's man-carrying glider, shown on the cover of the Mechanics' Magazine, 1852.

Mechanics' Magazine,

MUSEUM, REGISTER, JOURNAL, AND GAZETTE.

No. 1520.]   SATURDAY, SEPTEMBER 25, 1852.   [Price 3*d*., Stamped 4*d*.

Edited by J. C. Robertson, 166, Fleet-street.

SIR GEORGE CAYLEY'S GOVERNABLE PARACHUTES.

Fig. 2.

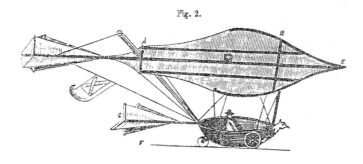

Fig. 1.

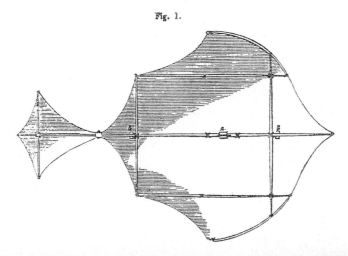

interest the careers of the first intrepid flyers and mechancis who came with their strange-looking machines. Within months of J W F Tranmer's letter of 2 May 1910 to Filey Urban District Council requesting permission for himself 'and other aviators to carry out experiments with aeroplanes on Filey Sands' a substantial hangar was erected on the Flat-Cliffs between Primrose Valley and Hunmanby Gap together with a concrete ramp to the beach. Remains of the ramp can still be seen on the cliff edge.[1]

The hangar was used to house and service the aircraft brought by rail to Filey, and when it was no longer employed for its original purpose it was taken down and rebuilt near Hunmanby Railway Station. Until relatively recently, older residents would refere to that part of Flat-Cliffs as 'near the hangar'. A bungalow built for the use of aviators and ground crews remains.[2]

Filey became the testing ground for the aircraft Company formed by Robert Blackburn in July 1910; the Blackburn Aircraft Company became one of the most successful aircraft companies of its day with a world-wide reputation.

Robert Blackburn was born in Leeds in 1885 and qualified in engineering before working in a local ironworks managed by his father. A tireless and diverse worker he was to become a pioneer in at least four fields - aviation, motor transport (he founded the Northern Automobile Company), motor sport, and radio. Developing an interest in aircraft design, one of his early machines was described as a 'winged four-poster bed!' Another model piloted by Bentfield C Huck was used on the beach by the Filey Flying School.

Bentfield C Hucks (Figure 4), another engineer was a test pilot for the Blackburn Aircraft Company, who had only just previously

Figure 4. B C Hucks in 1914 at Scarborough.

taught himself to fly at Filey. Later he was to become acknowledged to be the first English pilot to loop-the-loop, a manoeuvre which was then both difficult and dangerous; a report in a local newspaper in July 1914 described a loop he completed close to Filey Railway Station roof!

Possibly obsessed with speed, Hucks took up flying after being convicted of 'fast driving a motor car' which resulted in him losing his licence for three years.

Only 12 July 1911 he became the first person to pilot a heavier-than-air machine to Scarborough from Filey and land it. Scarborough was agog with excitement. Indeed, so many people crowded on to the south beach that evening that Hucks dared not risk taking off again and his aircraft, a Blackburn Mercury Mk II, was towed to the racecourse from where Hucks flew back to Filey - incidentally starting a long spell of using the racecourse as an airfield.

In March 1912, Robert Blackburn wrote from Balm Road, Leeds, to Filey UDC to point out the expense the aviators where incurring by maintaining an aviation centre at Filey and to confirm that they would have to move elsewhere if no financial support was made available to them. The aviators were keen to remin at Filey Bay as they wished to develop a hydroplane; however the members of the Council did not feel able to offer any assistance and so the short, but intensely interesting chapter of Filey's involvement in the early history of flying closed.

Along the coast, Scarborough was bitten by the flying bug very early in the development of aviation too, and was one of the first resorts to stage an Aviation Week which opened on Saturday 11 July 1914.

Many flyers came to Scarborough that week, but the undoubted star of the show was B C Hucks. By this time 'the death-defying looper'[3] had an aeroplane which had been specially made for peforming loop-the-loops by Louis Bleriot, the French airman who in July 1909 had become the first person to fly across the English Channel.

Unfortunately, Huck's 'looping machine' was not up to scratch for looping-the-loop during most of that Aviation Week, but Hucks, who seemed to spend much of his time giving flying demonstrations, and also earning extra money by taking people up for joy rides in his other aircraft, a two-seater, was by 1914 an accomplished showmen and crowd-pleaser and people were only too eager to overlook his lack of loop-the-loops.

The *Scarborough Evening News* reported that during the week B C Hucks repeatedly landed on both the south and north beaches to sell postcards[4] to the crowds and to pin on to buyers Aviation Week buttons, which were on sale at sixpence apiece!

To the delight of the crowds, Hucks did redeem his reputation as a 'death-defying looper' before he left Scarborough. He stayed in the town for several days after the close of Aviation Week and left on 23 July to give a display at Darlington. He was flying his repaired looping machine, and giving it a final test.

It obviously passed with flying colours, and he headed for his old testing ground at Filey where he did ten loops in succession. On the way back towards Scarborough Hucks completed another fifteen loops in succession - a record for successive loops. Then he did another eight in succession to set new personal record of thirty-three loops in one flight!

In the previous year, 1913, Scarborough had held its first Flying Festival. One of the stars of that event was another well-known French airman and record-breaker, Henri Salmet. He had won renown by setting a new record time for the flight between Paris and London. But Scarborough was to prove something of a jinx town for him.

In the days before World War I the *Daily Mail* newspaper was very keen on aviation. In addition to putting up huge cash prizes for the first pilots to accomplish certain flights, it sponsored flying exhibitions and shows including in 1912 the 'Daily Mail Waterplane Tour' organised by the Grahame White Aviation Company (Figure 5) which visited this part of England. It also sponsored individual pilots, contracting them to perform flying exhibitions in various parts of the country.

An enterprising Town Hall at Scarborough obviously saw a way of cashing in on the current craze for flying - and doing it on the cheap. The *Daily Mail* was persuaded to send Salmet, his Bleriot monoplane and his mechanics to Scarborough at the end of August 1913.

The Bleriot was based at the Racecourse and Henri Salmet gave daily demonstration flights over the South Bay. Scarborough may have got the French flyer cheaply thanks to the *Daily Mail*, but he was clearly no slouch when it came to making money. He took passengers up for short flights at four guineas a time. That was more than a working man would earn in a fortnight and was equivalent of more than today's cost of a return flight across the Atlantic.

It was during one of these passenger trips that the extremely low-flying Salmet had to swerve suddenly to avoid two women spectators on the Racecourse and crashed into a nearby coppice.

A photograph of the crashed plane shows that it had on its tail, beneath the French and British flags, the words 'entente cordiale'.

There was, in fact, it is reported, nothing at all cordial about the words Henri Salmet used as he and his passenger climbed uninjured from the battered machine. He put all the blame for the disaster on the two women bystanders in no uncertain terms.

The early years of flying, as we have seen, were not without danger to men and aircraft, and often to innocent bystanders. In August 1911, for instance, an aeroplane flew into a Miss E C Pimlott, of Hipperholme, Halifax, while she was on the beach at Filey. During Miss Pimlott's claim for damages at Leeds Town Hall she was represented by Mr A C Bairstow, KC, who described how she was swept into the air on a wing of the offending aeroplane and then thrown against the cliff. The jury awarded her £175 for her injuries which could well have been much more serious. The action was against Rupert Isaacson, a brilliant designer of engines who played a major role in building some of the first English aircraft. Frederick Handley Page and A V Roe, the founder of the Avro Aircraft Company, were two of the aviation pioneers who incorporated Isaacson's engines in their aeroplanes.[5]

Later that year, on 6 December a more serious accident took place when a Blackburn Mercury crashed, killing both the pilot, Hubert Oxley, and his passenger, Robert Weiss.[6]

Of the local air disasters hereabouts, perhaps the most famous,

Figure 5. An early seaplane on an East Coast beach during the Daily Mail Waterplane Tour of 1912.

was that which took place on 10 September 1937, when over a thousand spectators witnessed the death of two pilots who crashed at Scarborough while taking part in the famous King's Cup Air Race.

In the year of the crash the race was flown from Hatfield, up the East Coast via Scarborough where a turn was to be made to Newcastle, here the competing aircraft altered course for the finish at Baldonnel in Southern Ireland.

The two pilots were Wing-Commander P C Sherren, MC, who was forty-four, a Canadian who had served with the Canadian Infantry in France before being seconded to the Royal Flying Corp in May 1916. He was awarded the Military Cross and Bar for flying services in France and the India, General Medal with clasp for Waziristan 1921-24. Granted a permanent RAF Commission in 1919, he resigned from the Canadian Expeditionary Force, but was gazetted as a major in the Reserve of Officers Canadian Militia.

In November 1934 he was appointed to the Home Aircraft Depot, Henlow, for administrative duties. Previously he was in command of No.1 Armament Training Camp at Catfoss, Skipsea. It was he who had entered the aircraft, a Miles Falcon, and who was the official pilot.

The other man was a Londoner by birth, Wing-Commander Edward 'Ted' Hilton (41). He enlisted at eighteen at the outbreak of World War I. Commissioned to the East Yorkshire Regiment from the 14th Battalion London Regiment Territorial Force, he joined the RFC in France in 1917 as an observer. He was graded a pilot a year later, and from 1919 to 1923 was in Egypt and Iraq. Wing-Commander Hilton gained decorations for his war service and for his distinguished service in Kurdistan in 1923.

During his service with No.216 Squadron he commanded a flight from the unit which crossed Africa to Nigeria and West Africa in 1933. He was also one of a team of intrepid test pilots who put all machines, military and civil, through their paces before the Air Ministry certificate was granted. In 1936 delay at Athens robbed him of the chance to smash Amy Johnson's Cape record. As a serving test pilot at RAF Martlesham Heath, in Suffolk, his premature death held up the work he was engaged on by some months.

A *Scarborough Mercury* reporter in attendance at the King's Cup event at Scarborough, wrote the following account of the incident.

A thousand holidaymakers watching the King's Cup entrants pass the turning point on the Castle Hill were horrified to see the two occupants of a Miles Falcon flung out of their machine, one of them over the cliff side, when it nose-dived on to the top of the Castle Hill.

The machine which appeared about eleven o'clock, flew steadily over the town, but while making the turn towards the marking cross in the Castle Yard it appeared to receive a severe buffet from the strong gusty wind. The pilot seemed to loose control and the machine nose-dived into the ground. After hitting the ground one of the occupants was flung high into the air and landed fifty yards away, afterwards bouncing into the air a further fifty yards to the edge of the Castle Hill. He was still alive and could be seen vainly trying to grasp the wire fence which acts as a guard.

This he failed to do and amid a murmur of horror from the crowd he disappeared over the crest of the hill to fall to his death on the Marine Drive, three hundred feet below.

The other occupant was discovered, a headless corpse, thirty yards from where the machine hit the ground. He was a pitiful sight. The machine was completely wrecked, and the only part of it that was intact was the tail, upon which could still be seen the identification number 24.8

Coincidentally, an RAF pilot, Acting Pilot Officer George 'Lofty' Fraser, lost his life in a flying accident at Abusueir, in Egypt, the same day. He was flying a machine attached to No.4 Flying Training School.[9]

Incidentally, the winner of the 1937 King's Cup Air Race was Captain Percival, for a second year, who arrived at Baldonnel at 2.30pm and won the £200 prize for the fastest time for an aircraft exceeding 150 miles per hour. Percival's average speed from London to Dublin, excluding stops, was 225.2 mph. Captain Percival broke all records for the King's Cup. The previous highest speed record was his own 211 mph the previous year.

Charles E Gardiner, was second in the race, arriving twelve minutes later, despite engine trouble, on the way from Newtownards. Gardiner's average speed was 213.8 mph. Flying Officer Geoffrey R De Havilland won the second prize in Class "A".

Notes and References

1. Reardon, Michael Filey, *From Fishing Village to Edwardian Resort: The Story of Filey Through the Centuries,* Hutton Press, 1990.
2. *ibid.*
3. *Scarborough Evening News*
4. B C Hucks published his own postcards which carried a personalised logo; Figure 4 is an example of a Huck postcard issued by The B C Hucks Company, 166 Piccadilly, London.
5. Reardon.
6. *ibid.*
7. *Scarborough Mercury* Friday 10 September 1937. Inquest report 24 September.
8. *Scarborough Mercury* 10 September 1937.

6. Corn Windmills of Scarborough and District

by Edna Whelan

TOWERING OVER THE STREETS OF SCARBOROUGH is the tall bulk of a windmill (Figure 1). Fully restored with sails and fantail, it looms over the neighbouring tightly-packed terrace houses, and although no longer serving its original purpose, it nevertheless still provides a glimpse of the close proximity in which windmills and the people lived in previous centuries.

Now an award-winning hotel and restaurant, this brick-built mill dates from the early-nineteenth century on earlier foundations,[1] and stands just off Victoria Road, up Mill Street, and not far from the

town railway station. It was last owned by Mr Albert Prince Harrison, and before him, his father Moses Harrison, who lived nearby at *Calthorpe House*, Victoria Road (at the bottom of Mill Street) and today known as *Villa Marina*.[2]

Moses ran the mill in partnership with his brother Francis as a corn and seed merchant business, and it is thought Moses bought the windmill about 1850 from a Mr Harland, who later became connected with the Belfast shipbuilders, Harland and Wolff.[3] After being passed on to his son Albert, it continued in use until the autumn of 1927.[4] In latter days, however, it was fitted up with a twelve horse-power gas engine which drove the mill machinery.[5]

When Moses and Francis Harrison purchased the windmill it was then called Common Mill, but following the change of ownership, it became known as Harrison's Mill

Figure 1. The restored windmill at Scarborough, built in the nineteenth century. *Photograph by Alan Whitworth.*

Figure 2. Harrison's Mill, once called Common Mill, Mill Street, Victoria Road, about 1890.

(Figure 2). It is supposed that the mill was first erected around the year 1785 by Thomas Robinson. In 1796 it was owned by a Dr Belcombe, who had it off a Mr Jack Binns.

A former employee at the mill, Mr Charles Ditchburn, who started work at the mill aged fourteen and earned fifteen shillings per week, said that 'a huge wooden shaft ran up the centre of the windmill from a five ton cherry-wood wheel. Wooden cogs drove the iron wheels which, in turn, powered the stone grinding machinery' and that 'once a week the whole assembly had to be lifted up on two huge bottle-jacks so that the phosphor-bronze cup in which the central shaft rested, could be oiled.'[6]

In nineteenth century Scarborough, it is said that 'the sails of four windmill stood out against the sky'[7] - Greengate Mill at the foot of Mill Street, North Marine Road (Greengate Lane is the old name for North Marine Road); Albion Mill on the North Cliffe, which was demolished sometime after 1860 for the erection of Osborne House, now part of Gibson's Hotel[8] - this was a tower windmill with four sails shown on Wood's map of 1828 and seen on an engraving of the Seaman's Hospital (Figure 3); the Common Mill (Mill Street, Victoria Road) often called Harrison's Mill; and one on the South Cliffe where St Martin's church stands.[9]

Figure 3. Nineteenth century engraving of the Seaman's Hospital, Scarborough, showing Albion Mill on the left.

This mill was first recorded in 1523 and mentioned again in 1556.[10] Earlier, in 1320, 'a windmill belonging to the Crown' may have been this mill.[11] Interestingly, in 1660-61, it is recorded that 'the inhabitants [of Scarborough] knew of only one windmill, pulled down in the Civil War' - a statement possibly suggestive that more than one windmill stood in the early seventeenth century.[12]

Mention of John Wood's map published in 1828, reminds me that another windmill occupied a site on North Cliffe off the Whitby Road not far from Albion Mill and in direct line of vision behind the Seaman's Hospital on the engraving mentioned above, thus possibly bringing the total number of windmills standing in that century to five. Also it is probable that a windmill stood at Cloughton at some period, as undoubtedly Mill Lane refers to a road which lead to a mill, although at what date is not known, but Moses Harrison was the son of William Harrison who farmed at Cloughton in the early days of the nineteenth century and it is said that Moses used to carry a hundredweight sack of corn on his shoulder from Cloughton to Scarborough Market on Thursdays to sell to the millers for grinding into flour or as 'grist'.[13] This then suggests that the windmill predates this century.

Lastly, on he subject of Scarborough windmills. In Sotheran's *Scarborough Guide* of 1787, a windmill is said to have been erected about this date mentioned in short passage which reads :

> *Bread, at Scarborough, has been humorously pronounced the wholesomest in England, as being lighter . . . than that of most corporate towns; by some ounces in the sixpenny loaf! But it must also be observed, that wheat is, upon an average, dearer here than at the neighbouring markets; and so, in proportion of about a seventh until the late building and establishment, of that ample windmill, which now supplies, and decorates the town.*

To which mill the writer is referring is not known, but it may be Common Mill on Victoria Road which is thought to have been put up around this period.

It is said that there were seven windmills between Bridlington and Whitby; all of brick and which had been coated with tar on the outside 'to preserve them'. These were built on stone foundations.[14] Whatever the truth of this statement at one time, the number of windmills was probably considerably higher. For instance, three stood in Whitby town alone during the nineteenth century, and another eight or nine could be found in the villages roundabout (Figure 4).

The earliest mention of a windmill in Whitby occurs in the year 1316 connected with the abbey. In all probability, this mill, which Charlton erroneously describes at one point as a gold-mill,[15] was the one sited at Sneaton, granted to the abbot by Alexander de Percy.[16] The spot where the windmill stood was possibly an eminence about a mile above the village still known by the name of Windmill Hill (OS 6" 1851), and it may be supposed to have been the first windmill in the district.[17] In 1394, the site of a mill, Windmill Flatt, is recorded a little east of Whitby Abbey.[18] This undoubtedly is the same mill as that mentioned in 1540 on the east cliff near the monastery,[19] and may be one of two windmills conveyed to Richard Cholmley in 1557[20] by John York who had them off the Earl of Warwick in 1551.[21]

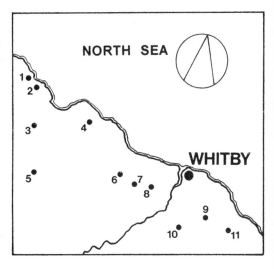

1. Port Mulgrave 2. Hinderwell 3. Ellerby
4. Goldsborough 5. Ugthorpe 6. Dunsley
7. Newholm 8. Stakesby 9. Stainsacre
10. Sneaton 11. Hawsker

Figure 4. A map of the windmill sites of Whitby and district. *Drawn by Alan Whitworth.*

The exact location of either windmill is not given, and it may be that one refers to a mill which stood at Low Hawsker, as the document records the conveyance of lands and manors among which is listed Hawsker,[22] where a windmill shell survives to this day.

In 1577 a windmill is recorded in the hamlet of Dunsley (parish of Whitby).[23] Sir Hugh Cholmley's marriage settlement to Lady Anne Compton, dated 26 April 1666 mentions a windmill at Whitby,[24] and in 1674 a windmill in the parish of Whitby was leased for one year.[25]

By 1677 it is obvious that more than one windmill stood in the town, as a document which, while mentioning Windmill Flatts in its conveyance of 'all that messuage or tenement with the closes of arable meadow and pasture in the tenure of Lambert Russell being reputed part of Windmill Flatts', is more interesting in its reference to 'the windmill within the manor of Whitby' and at the same time, to another windmill whose location is not given.[26]

During the eighteenth century, some windmills not already in existence sprang up about the Whitby district, and it may be at this time too, that a number of the former were rebuilt, as earlier windmills would have been wooden post-mills with an average life-span of around forty or fifty years.[27]

Certainly windmills at Hinderwell and Ugthorpe can be dated to this period, as can that at Stakesby; known variously as Fletcher's Mill, Arundel Mill or Anderson's Mill. Mentioned in a conveyance document of October 1778, it was a 'Wind Corn Mill' in the ownership of Elizabeth Knaggs and James Lewis, and was probably the corn mill referred to in a mortgage release dated 28 May 1796. In another conveyance dated 4 August 1863 a windmill and site at Stakesby is again noted, Wind Mill Hill Field and a George Fletcher is given as the miller.[28]

In an advertisement in the *Whitby Gazette* of 27 March 1869, a windmill is 'for let, and may be entered upon the 13th day of May next, the WIND MILL at Stakesby, near Whitby, together with the HOUSE and GRANARIES; also a GRASS FIELD, and a large GARDEN; For rent and particulars apply to Mr William Ruff, Stakesby, Whitby.'

The corn mill at Lower Stakesby, which the local Whitby historian Reverend George Young mentions was in his time in the occupation of Mr T Anderson, and had previously been an oil-mill, was pulled down in 1877.[29] It was stated the site of the mill formed part of the garden of a house named *Arundel Howe* erected by Edward H Smales in the same year, consequently, there may have been more than one windmill in Stakesby as certainly in a conveyance dated 20 June 1898, a 'messuage and Dwelling House, Wind Corn Mill, Granaries and Close . . . Wind Mill Field . . . situated at or near Lower Stakesby' clearly cannot have been the one demolished in 1877 unless it had been replaced.[30]

Anderson's Mill at Stakesby is illustrated in Gaskin's, *The Old Seaport of Whitby,* and may be described as a circular tower mill of three-storey. The cap, while not quite the traditional boat shape common to this area, is very similar and shows clearly the endless chain attachment which operates the rocking lever mechanism that adjusts the shutters on the four 'patent' sails.[31]

The windmill at Ugthorpe (Figure 5) was erected in 1796 on the site of an earlier structure. Again, this was a fixed tower mill, similar in profile to Anderson's Mill but sported an automatic fan-wheel at the rear for turning the moveable cap into the wind. In 1860, the mill was offered for sale and an advertisement to the effect appeared in the *Whitby Gazette.*[32]

It is possible that at this point the mill was taken over by a Mr C Walker, as a local bill-head for 1872 displays his name as 'Miller and Corn Manufacturer'.[33] Ugthorpe Mill was again under new management in 1889, when Robert Dobson bought the mill and adjoining cottage for £105. He worked the mill until his death in 1906 whereupon his son, Robert inherited the windmill, valued then at £150. By 1934, Robert Dobson, Jnr, had in turn rented the structure to a miller named Wilkinson, for an annual rent of fifteen pounds. At the death of Robert Dobson, Jnr, the windmill was taken over by Eric Stonehouse, of Wakefield.[34] Today Ugthorpe Mill still stands, visible from the main moorland road to Gusiborough, and is converted to holiday accommodation (Figure 6).

Known as the Royal George Mill, the windmill at Hinderwell which stood up until the middle of this century, possibly had its origins in the eighteenth century. The exact date of the first mill is not known, but local tradition as it, that it was in the year 1805 when it was converted to a steam-driven windmill with the addition of an engine house and chimney adjoining - however, it may have been later when this occurred, as one source gives a date of 1870.[35] An inscribed stone on the side of the building recorded it was built by Isaac Moon. The Moon family were local millers who also worked Dalehouse water-mill. When Isaac died in 1842, he left his estate including the windmill to his son, George Moon, who con-tinued to work it for some years.

Figure 5. The cap and sails of Ugthorpe windmill c.1946.

Extremely tall, it stood seven-storeys high, and was powered by four sails and contained two pairs of French millstones and cylinders. In the 1860s, in an effort to improve business perhaps, consideration was given to forming the mill into a co-operative, and shares in the mill were offered

Figure 6. Ugthorpe Mill today, now converted to holiday accommodation. *Photograph by Alan Whitworth.*

for sale. Notice was duly posted in the Whitby Gazette of 31 October 1868:

> *...It having been considered by many persons desirable to convert the above property into a UNION MILL in five pound ordinary shares. A MEETING will be held at the Shoulder of Mutton Inn, Hinderwell, on Tuesday, the 3rd of November, 1868, at six o'clock in the evening, when all are respectfully invited to attend.*
>
> *The utility of these Mills is now generally admitted to be a great benefit to every neighbourhood where they are established, as well as a useful and safe investment.*

Wm HARRISON, Auctioneer.

Whether it became a Union Mill is not known, but in January 1873 it was mentioned in a conveyance, noted as a 'Wind Corn Mill with Steam Mill' and having 'two granaries'. Operations at the mill ceased sometime before the turn of the century, with the machinery being removed around 1915.

A former Hinderwell resident, Mr John Sanderson, recalls how his 'late aunt, Mrs Lyth, used to tell how they had dances on the floor of the old windmill and one very windy night they had just left for home when the sails of the mill fell to the ground and they had a fortunate escape.'[36]

In Whitby itself, little is known about the number and location of the earlier windmills which may have survived into the eighteenth century, or indeed, about any which may have been erected during this period. However, in the year 1800, Union Mill was built, and on Wood's map of 1828 three windmills were shown to be in existence, one of which was Anderson's Mill mentioned previously, and one of which was also shown on a later Ordnance Survey map and named 'Bagdale Windmill (Corn)'.

It is possible that this latter mill at Bagdale, may have come into existence during the eighteenth century. Like Stakesby windmill, it too had numerous names, variously called Noble's Mill, Wren's Mill and Burnett's Mill, after its owners. Demolished in 1862, it was last owned by a Mr Chapman, with George Burnett being the last tenant for about eight years, he himself leaving in 1861. He is mentioned in a conveyance dated 17 April 1857 which reads in part, 'all that Wind Corn Mill and messuage cottage or dwelling-houses situated in or near Bagdale...now in the occupation of GEO. BURNETT and also two closes in or near Bagdale called BAGDALE MILL FIELD containing 6a 1r 11p and BAGDALE FAR FIELD containing 7a 2r 10p'. Before him was Mr Wren.

Illustrated in Gaskin it is seen as a small, circular windmill, three-storeys high, with straight sides unlike the majority which have a taper. Also, unlike others in the district, Wren's Mill had a depressed Dutch ogee-shaped cap. Interestingly, it is depicted as having four sails, yet in a print published in 1842 by J F Howard, which shows clearly the 'three mills' of Whitby, Wren's Mill seen in the foreground has six sails![37]

The site of Wren's Mill is given by Gaskin as standing beside 'the west side of the North Eastern Railway, between Whitby Town and West Cliff stations, opposite the back of the Roman Catholic convent since erected near Chubb Hill Road' an area known as Mill Factory Field.[38] A more detailed description reads, 'to the left of the path up Stakesby Fields, after crossing the North Eastern Railway bridge, are some piggeries and cowhouses in a field in the occupation of Mr Walshaw. These are partially built of old material of the mill. The mill stood in direct line between these piggeries and the railway line (6yds to piggeries, 10yds to railway line). There was just sufficient room for the mill wings to revolve between the mill building and the piggeries.'[39]

The foundation stone of the Whitby Union Mill was laid on the 16 June 1800, and on a pottery mug produced to commemorate the event (Figure 7) an inscription runs, 'From Stormy Blasts and Dangers ill May God Protect the Union Mill', a sentiment which served well for eighty years until 1880, when a storm on 5 October blew off the roof.

Formed as the Union Mill Industrial and Provident Society Limited, Young, states how:

It was set on foot by liberal benefactions, including a legacy of £100

Figure 7. Union Mill Commemorative Mug with inscription taken from the reverse side, which can be seen in the Whitby Museum, Pannett Park. *Drawn by Alan Whitworth.*

left by Mrs Hancock, yet it is more properly a trading company than a charity; each of the members, whose number amounts to about 900, enjoying a share in the profits of the concern, by obtaining flour at a reduced price. The wind-mill and premises belonging to this society form a conspicuous object on the west side of Whitby. For fourteen years, the business was conducted by Mr John Watson, president, and a committee annually renewed, composed of gentlemen who had taken an active part in founding the society, with other benevolent characters, under whose skilful management, all the heavy debts contracted at the erection of the mill were paid off, and the institution, freed of all incumbrance, was brought to yield a substantial benefit to the members. At the beginning of 1815, a revolution took place in the society, attended with circumstances over which he historian would wish to throw a veil. Suffice it to remark, that the treatment which Mr Watson and others received after long, arduous, and disinterested labours, illustrates a well known truth that he who serves the public, must serve it from a sense of duty, rather than from the hope of gratitude. In both its periods, the mill seems to have answered its principal design, of furnishing good and cheap flour for the use of a great part of the inhabitants of Whitby.[40]

A footnote here, goes on to remark, 'The society has been very unfortunate in its rules, the original rules being in some parts defective, and liable to abuse, while those now acted upon are partly tyrannical and partly puerile.'[41]

Despite the possibility of mismanagement, Unions Mills, however, flourished throughout England during the late-nineteenth century, and as we have already observed, the miller of Hinderwell at one time thought the idea attractive enough to consider.

Notices of a 'share out' were given periodically in the *Whitby Gazette* among other sources, and a typical advertisement to that effect is given below :

UNION MILL INDUSTRIAL & PROVIDENT SOCIETY LTD

On Tuesday, February 14th, the Committee will attend the Mill from Nine o'clock in the morning until Four o'clock in the Afternoon, to deliver to each member A STONE OF BEST FLOUR, on producing their Ticket. One penny per stone will be charged to pay Meal Sellers for their attendance, and for defraying the incidental expenses. Members omitting to attend on the above mentioned day, may receive their flour on the Wednesday, Thursday, or Friday, following, by applying to the President with their Tickets, and paying sixpence extra for each stone. It is required by the Committee that every Ticket be registered in the name of the present owner; and it is requested, that any person intending to purchase a ticket, should previously ascertained from the President, if it is properly registered.

Whitby, Feb 3rd, 1860 R. HORNE, PRESIDENT

A surviving example of a share-holders ticket (Figure 8) displays a remarkable facet of English folk-lore worth describing. An examination reveals curious little punch marks, square-shaped along the upper edge. They denote how many times it was used and led to the saying - 'having been through the mill'.

On 11 July 1888, the Union Mill Society was wound up and soon after, the windmill unroofed in a storm earlier that year, and the ancillary buildings were sold off. Later, in 1912, the mill was bought and converted by the Territorial Army Association into stables and gun rooms. An extremely prominent landmark in the town, Union Mill differed from others in having five sails. The site today is occupied by Harrison's Garage, at the top of Chubb Hill Road.

Other windmills which surrounded Whitby included one at Skelder,[42] one at Newholm, and another at Stainsacre, mentioned in a conveyance dated 14 July 1888, which described, 'all that WIND CORN MILL with the piece of ground whereon the same stands and thereunto belonging to, and also that messuage or dwelling house, granary and outbuildings nearby adjoining the mill'; today, only the name *Windmill Inn* recalls the existence of this mill. These windmills probably date from the nineteenth century, as did the stone-built mill at Ravenscar (Figure 9), bearing the date 1858 carved into its plinth, which was offered for sale when first erected in this manner :

MILLER WANTED for a new windmill at Peak, near Stainton Dale, at Scarborough. He must be a steady, industrious man with a good character, and one who thoroughly

Figure 8. Union Mill Ticket No.502, once belonging to George Gibson. Notice the punch-marks around the top edge (see above).

Figure 9. Peak Mill, Ravenscar, erected in 1858 and today a derelict shell. *Photograph by Alan Whitworth.*

understands his business. If with a wife that could take charge of a small Inn, built near the Mill, it would be preferred. Apply by letter, with terms, to Mr Hammond, Raven Hall, near Scarborough.[43]

Of earlier date, were the windmills at Normanby and Raithwaite, both shown on Thomas Jeffery's map of 1772, and a windmill existed at Mulgrave in the nineteenth century, as did one at Ellerby, both of which possibly had earlier origins.

Though sadly no longer gracing the roadside of the A171 at Selly Hill, some two miles west of Whitby, the millhouse of Newholm windmill (Figure 10) still survives. On some older maps it is shown as 'Burnt Mill'. At what point it ceased operations is unclear, but certainly by 1935 it was disused and under the ownership of Sir John Harrowing, who allowed its inspection at that time for the purposes of recording the mill with a view to proposing its preservation along with the other eight or nine reported to exist in the district at that date.[44]

Concerning nineteenth century windmills, of those previously mentioned, Hawsker or Low Hawsker Mill is possibly the only one in the area which can trace its ancestry to the medieval period. Notwithstanding that, however, the structure which survives to this day dates only from the late-nineteenth century, being either built or rebuilt in brick sometime in the mid-1800s by a Mr Burnett and his nephew John Burnett.

The production of ground corn here ceased dramatically, however, in August 1868, although albeit following the events described in the *Whitby Times* of 4 September 1868, and reproduced below, it is evident

Figure 10. A drawing of Newholm Mill, near Whitby, by Margaret L. Clark, from a photograph. *Reproduced from the Victoria County History, North Yorkshire, Vol. II.*

that a windmill was restored or entirely rebuilt and milling continued; but by 1935, when Karl Wood, the noted windmill artist painted Hawsker Mill, it was described as derelict.[45]

On Tuesday last, Hawsker Mill was completely destroyed by fire. The mill was a solid structure, built of brick only a few years ago and was carried on by Mr George Burnett, the owner, who resided in the adjoining house, which communicated with the mill.

On Monday night, Mr Burnett was grinding corn in the mill until 10 o'clock. He fastened up the premises a little after ten, having with him when he did so a candle, the flame of which was exposed, and may have led to the conflagration. He then went to bed, but between one and two in the morning, he awoke, fancying that he saw a blaze, he got up and discovered that the mill was enveloped in flames.

He immediately raised an alarm, and a young man was despatched on horseback to Whitby for assistance. Mr George Buchannan, the agent for the Yorkshire Insurance Office, in which the property was insured, was communicated with, the result was that a fire engine, drawn by two horses, and accompanied by the fire brigade, proceeded to the scene of the conflagration.

On arrival, they found that the flames had made great progress, and caused much havoc; the interior of the mill, with all it contained, being entirely destroyed. The dwelling-house and sheds were in imminent danger, but by prompt and vigorous use of an adequate supply of water, the fire was arrested, and the residence saved from injury, but the cart-shed, stable, and granary, which adjoined he mill, were burnt down. There was a great quantity of flour and wheat in the mill, which were destroyed, as were also the machinery and other effects therein.

About six in the morning, the fire was nearly subdued, and the mill-wands fell and were broken to pieces. Two stacks of hay close to were saved, the fire being prevented from reaching them. The fire may be said to have burnt itself out, and ended in the complete destruction of the mill, and buildings and property mentioned. The damage is estimated at £1000. The owner's loss by the destruction of his mill and buildings is covered by an insurance in the Yorkshire Office, but his stock-in-trade we hear, is only partially insured. We understand the adjoining house was not insured.

Mr Superintendent Clarkson, Sergeant Martindale, and several constables were in attendance, and rendered effective aid. The origin of the fire has not yet been ascertained.

Finally, elsewhere within the Scarborough borough boundary, windmills have been recorded at Gristhorpe, where a mill was first mentioned as early as 1314, recorded again in 1595,46 and which still stood in 1732 when sails for the windmill cost 15s 0d.[47] This mill stood on high ground to the north of the village, and east of the road to Falsgrave.

Another early windmill was first mentioned in 1298 at Hunmanby as belonging to Robert de Tateshale, and worth 40s.[48] By 1600 there were two windmills here.[49] In 1635 they were known as Old Mill and Gardiner Mill, and owned by William Leppington, who attempted to enforce a 'suit of mill-soke' upon Charles Stutville and other inhabitants,[50] which resulted in the provision of bye-laws for the proper conduct of the miller being drawn up and included in the Court of Pain at Hunmanby in 1732.[51] In 1772, however, only a single windmill was shown on Jeffery's map, standing west of the village near the Folkton road, but a century later just before 1830, a

Figure 11. Little Smeaton Post-mill c.1960. This was a type of wooden windmill similar to one of the mills which stood at Muston which survived until 1826. *Photograph courtesy of the Muggeridge Collection.*

second mill was erected on the Bartindale road. Two millers were recorded in White's Directory of 1858,[52] but the newer windmill had apparently gone out of use by 1872.[53] The older mill ceased operations shortly before 1909[54] and was in a derelict state by 1935,[55] and no trace of either windmill remained by 1970.

From 1341 onwards a windmill was frequently mentioned at Muston.[56] In 1575 two windmills were recorded[57] one of which survived in the form of a wooden post-mill (Figure 11) until 1826.[58] This was marked on Jeffery's map of 1772. Later, in the nineteenth century a new windmill was built of brick to replace the mills lost which was derelict by 1935,[59] and the stump of this remains to this day (Figure 12) on the road into Filey, often misguidedly thought to be the windmill belonging to Filey.

At Filey itself, a windmill was recorded in the sixteenth century[60] and in the nineteenth century a wind corn-mill stood in Common Right Road. A miller was last recorded in 1892.[61] While at Reighton, a windmill was first mentioned in 1580,[62] and again in 1635,[63] which remained until last recorded in 1713.[64]

Today, few windmills survive in any state of completeness, and only rarely in the north of England do we come across any working; only at Skidby, is there a fully-restored operating windmill in Yorkshire, a sad indictment for a structure that was once so common in the landscape of Scarborough and district.

Figure 12. Muston Mill, near Filey as it stands today. *Photograph by Alan Whitworth.*

Notes and References

1. *Scarborough Evening News,* 31 August 1984.
2. *ibid.*
3. *Scarborough Mercury,* 7 October 1955.
4. *Scarborough Evening News,* 31 August 1984.
5. *ibid,* 17 November 1977.
6. *ibid.*
7. Rowntree, Arthur *History of Scarborough*, 1931.
8. Berryman, B *Scarborough As It Was,* 1977.
9. Rowntree, *A History of Scarborough*, 1931.
10. Yorkshire Archaeological Society, Yorkshire Feet of Fines, Tudor Period. 15 Hen. VIII; 2 & 3 Philip & Mary.
11. YAS, Rentals & Surveys (Gen. Series), Bdle.17, No.52.
12. Exchequer Department, 12 & 13 Chas.II, No.1.
13. *Scarborough Evening News,* 31 August 1984.
14. *Scarborough Mercury,* 7 October 1977.
15. Charlton, L *History of Whitby and Whitby Abbey,* 1799.

16. Young, Rev George *History of Whitby*, 1817.
17. *ibid.*
18. *ibid.*
19. L & P Hen.VIII, 15, No.565.
20. YAS, Yorkshire Feet of Fines, Tudor Period, Vol.1, 1573.
21. *ibid*, 5 Edw.VI.
22. *ibid.*
23. *ibid*, Tudor Period, Vol.1, 1573.
24. Whitby Literary & Philosophical Society Papers.
25. *ibid.*
26. *ibid.*
27. *Yorkshire Archaeological Journal*, Vol.45, 1977.
28. Whitby Lit. & Phil. Soc. Papers.
29. Young, Rev George *History of Whitby*, 1817.
30. Whitby Lit. & Phil. Soc. Papers.
31. Gaskin, R T The *Old Seaport of Whitby*, 1909.
32. *Whitby Gazette*, September 1935; Whitworth, A. *Yorkshire Windmills*, 1991.
33. Whitby Lit. & Phil. Soc. Papers.
34. *Whitby Gazette*, September 1935.
35. Burns, T *Round and About the North Yorkshire Moors*, 1987.
36. *ibid.*
37. Humble, A F *Prints of Old Whitby*, nd.
38. Gaskin, R T The *Old Seaport of Whitby*, 1909.
39. Whitby Lit. & Phil. Soc. Papers.
40. Young, Rev George *History of Whitby*, 1817.
41. *ibid.*
42. *Whitby Gazette*, September 1935.
43. ibid, 2 October 1858, reproduced in Whitworth, A. *Yorkshire Windmills*, 1991.
44. *Whitby Gazette*, September 1935.
45. Wilson, C *Checklist of Windmill Paintings of Karl Wood*, 1982. Lincs. Museum Occasional Papers No.1
46. YAS, YFF, Tudor Period, Vol.II, 37 Eliz.I.
47. *History of Gristhorpe*, 1998.
48. YAS, Yorkshire Inquisitions Post Mortem, Vol.VI, p67.
49. ERRO, DDHU/9/32, 38.
50. E 134/11 Chas.I.
51. ERRO, DDHU/10/81, No.4-7.
52. White, William *Directory of York and the North Riding*, 1858.
53. Kelly's *Directory of the North & East Riding of Yorkshire*, 1872, p509; OS 6" 1893.
54. ibid, 1909; OS 6" 1909.
55. Wilson, C *Checklist of the Windmill Paintings of Karl Wood*, 1982.
56. Cal. Inq. PM viii, p273; BM Add.MS 26718 f.36d; Cal.Pat. 1553-4, 85-6; Yorks Fines 1614-25, p122.
57. YAS, YFF, 17 Eliz.I.
58. ERRO, Regy. Deeds DY/113/139.
59. Wilson, C. *Checklist of Windmill Paintings of Karl Wood*, 1982.
60. ERRO, E 310/28/168 f.29.
61. Baines, W. *Directory of Yorkshire, East Riding*, 1892, p185.
62. YAS, YFF, 22 & 23 Eliz.I.
63. E 134/11 Chas.II. Mich.53
64. ERRO, Regy. Deeds E/167/286.

7. Ship Carvings in Whitby Parish Church

by Dr Andrew White

WHITBY PARISH CHURCH is quite exceptional and unlike any other church in England. From its cliff-top position it dominates not only the town and harbour below, but also a very extensive parish. Formerly its parish was even more extensive - in 1851 it covered 15,918 acres[1] - and the people trooped each Sunday from surrounding villages such as Sleights and Ugglebarnby, or from the scattered farms of Eskdaleside, to take their places in township pews in the transepts, while the townsfolk of Whitby itself struggled up the 199 steps to sit in the nave or in the many galleries. These were the days of frequent and lengthy services, with marathon sermons timed by an hour-glass.

The burgeoning population of Whitby was installed at first in the nave, but from just before the year 1700[2] in an ever-increasing series of galleries running all around the church, not excluding the chancel arch itself, which is bridged by the grandest pew of all, the Cholmley Pew, erected by the seventeenth century owners of the former Abbey estates.[3] This is symbolic of the power and arrogance of the squirearchy, who could do almost whatever they wanted. When the north side of the church was extended in 1819 and it reached its greatest capacity, it is said that some 2,500 people could be seated in the church of St Mary[4] (Figure 1).

It is the variety and complexity of the pews and galleries, in a plain, no-nonsense domestic Georgian style of carpentry, that gives

Figure 1. The inside of St Mary's church, Whitby, showing a glimpse of the numerous pews and galleries which fill the interior. *Photograph by Alan Whitworth.*

the church its special charm. The late Sir Nikolaus Pevsner accorded it a rare tribute, saying, 'It is one of the churches one is fondest of in the whole of England'[5] and likewise, Alec Clifton Taylor was equally complimentary.[6] Not surprising it was an anathema to the Victorians and one nineteenth century rector of the town went so as far as to state, '[It is] now perhaps the most depraved sacred building in the kingdom.'[7]

The pews and galleries are of great variety. The former range from snug solid affairs of mahogany lined with green or red baize for the comfort of merchant and ship-owning families, to plain painted or varnished deal for others. A carefully hierarchial order of society is commemorated in the pews, and a number of names and dates, particularly in the galleries of the south transept, record owners going back to the mid-eighteenth century. Pews were private property and could be left by will, or sold.

If the cushioned and baize-lined pews of the prosperous promoted sleep during the lengthy services of the eighteenth and nineteenth centuries, then the hard pews of those less well-off promoted more wakeful activities. The seats themselves, the book ledges, the ends and the fronts of many pews bear witness to a long-continued graffito industry. In particular, the fronts of pews, below the book ledge, were ideally placed for careful carving where the kneeling artist could get to work out of sight of the pulpit.

While the majority of graffiti undoubtedly consists merely of dates and initials, there are many more interesting types. There are a number of human figures (Figure 2), while in the south transept numerous simple buildings are depicted, usually with prominent flags on the roofs. These often enclose sets of initials and dates, including some very early ones from the mid-seventeenth century.

Fascinating as these are, however, I wish to concentrate here upon the graffiti of ships, of which there are at least forty-three examples scattered about the church. No less than seven of these are to be found in the first pew of the east gallery, just to the north of the Cholmley pew.

Ship graffiti are not uncommon in churches and several earlier ships are depicted at Marton, in Lincolnshire, and

Figure 2. An unidentified head, one of the many human figures carved into the pews of the parish church. *Rubbing by Alan Whitworth.*

at Cley-next-to-the-Sea on the Norfolk coast, for instance and St Ninian's church in Whitby also preserves a few graffiti of ships in the pews of the west gallery.[8] However, I am not aware of any other church in the country which contains so many graffiti of ships of the eighteenth and nineteenth centuries. A large factor in this is undoubtedly the preservation of the old pews here at St Mary's when so many elsewhere were discarded during Victorian restorations.

Figure 3. East Gallery, Pew 1. A sloop. The hull with ports and possibly a raised quarter-deck. Of interest is the Union Flag set somewhat archaically from the martingale.

No resident of Whitby in the period from 1700 to 1900 could fail to be impressed by the number of sailing ships to be seen in the harbour.[9] It was, moreover, a sight which for a great many people immediately preceded their visit to church on Sunday. A significant number of those worshipping in the parish church also gained their livelihood either directly, or indirectly from shipping. Shipowners, shipbuilders, sailmakers, riggers, seamen and fishermen all had an interest and most of them enough technical knowledge to produce passable illustrations of sailing vessels, even if they lacked the artistry to make them entirely convincing. Some of these worshippers were clearly too 'respectable' to carve graffiti into church pews. So who did?

Figure 4. East Gallery, Pew 1. A sloop. The hull with ports. A raked mast and shrouds or backstays. The topsail is rather odd-shaped. This also could be an attempt at a revenue cutter.

We shall never know for certain, but the fact that the graffiti can only be found in the plainer pews of the church suggests that those who carved them came from among the poorer people of the parish, perhaps the seamen, fishermen, and particularly the boys and young men, many of them apprenticed to the sea in some way.

At the end of the eighteenth and beginning of the nineteenth centuries, it was the whaling vessels which were the

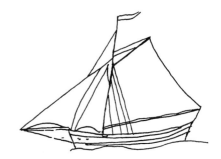

Figure 5. East Gallery, Pew 1. A sloop, very competently carved, and along with Fig.9 the most artistic of the garffiti. The mast has shrouds or backstays and the low rig spread out probably represents a trading vessel of the type which served the alum works along the coast.

most prominent in the harbour; they were laid up for long periods in the winter, until the spring thaw unlocked the Arctic ice.[10] At other times, more common were the bluff and solid collier barks, cats and brigs, many of them built and owned in Whitby. However, once launched, these were relatively infrequent visitors to the port itself, spending most of their lives on the regular run from the Tyne or Wear to London, returning in ballast.[11]

Figure 6. East Gallery, Pew 1. A brigantine rather than a schooner, on the evidence of the jibs and staysails. As usual the rigging is a good deal more detailed than the hull.

Figure 7. South Transept Gallery, Pew behind I. Holt's Pew, 1750. A very fragmentary though interesting graffito. It could be one of the oldest, although topgallant masts seem to be shown. It depicts a three-masted square-rigger, either a barque or ship-rigged. Like many of the graffiti it demonstrates the difficulty of representing square sails convincingly from abeam.

Figure 8. North Transept, West End, 4th Set, Front Pew. A small sloop, its hull with ports and apparently containing two seated figures. A multiplicity of jacks adorn the yards.

Other, smaller types of craft regularly seen in the harbour would have been the small coasting schooners and brigantines, fishing-boats, including the characteristic cobles, and pilot-boats. Small sloops of about fifty tonnes were very popular in the local alum trade, because they had to beach on the rocky shores to load alum and unload coal at the works. It is not surprising, therefore, that it is schooners and brigantines among the larger vessels and sloops among the smaller which appear most frequently among the graffiti.[12]

It is noteworthy that several graffiti show what may be the same vessel; one with a very lofty rig, perhaps representing a revenue cutter or pilot boat.[13] Whatever it is, it seems to have caught the attention and imagination of a number of people, just as a fast or powerful car would today. Strangely enough, no local coble boats seem to be represented and for that matter, only one paddle-steamer and one screw steamer have been noted. A curiously childish carving of a rowing-boat in the nave has the elementary mistake of depicting the rowers seated the wrong way round! It could represent a naval barge, or possibly a gig of the type traditionally raced in the Whitby Regatta.

With one exception, it is impossible to

put a close date on these graffiti. They seem to range from the eighteenth to the early twentieth century. Of course, the pews and galleries themselves offer some sort of *terminus post quem* - in other words, the graffiti are unlikely to be earlier than the pew they are cut into. On the other hand, we do not know how much later they may be.

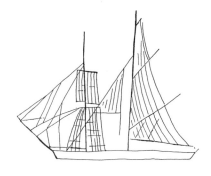

To take an example, graffiti in the north extension cannot be earlier than 1819[14] but some of the seating here may be up to fifty years later. Furthermore, there are clear signs that a number of pews have been altered, repaired or even moved around the church over the centuries; panels removed from one may have been used in another pew. One of the pews in the north gallery, for instance, has as its back part of an earlier pew with its owner's name on it, but turned through ninety degrees. Other clues come to our aid, however, and judging by a long series of dates and initials cut into the pews of the extended north transept, these pews were not installed until the last quarter of the nineteenth century, so the ship carvings on these are, correspondingly, unlikely to be any earlier.

Figure 9. Nave, South Side, Pew 5. Along with Fig.5 this is one of the finest carvings in the church, of a brigantine. While not all its rigging is entirely convincing the overall effect is very spirited and striking. The shrouds and mainsail on the foremast seem to have become confused. The mainsail has multiple gaff topsails (Scale 2/3).

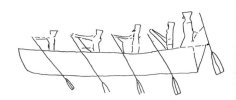

Figure 10. Nave, Pew 5. Childish carving of a rowing gig or galley with four oarsmen and a fifth sailor working a steering oar over the stern. The oarsmen appear to be using two oars each, but are facing the wrong way round! (Scale 2/3)

A large number of graffiti appear unfinished. Perhaps the sermon ended abruptly, or the artist was over-ambitious in his composition, or lacked the staying power to complete his carving, or was, more simply, caught and admonished. At all events, these simple graffiti, cut probably with no more assistance than a clasp-knife and a prayer book as a straight-edge, often show an amazing economy of line and have the capacity to speak more directly to us of the interests and preoccupations of past generations of ordinary Whitby folk, than do much more

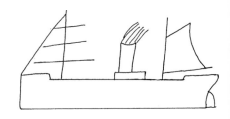

Figure 11. East Gallery, Pew 1. Steam and sail. A small coaster with indications of a square-rigged mainmast and a gaff mizen. Last quarter of the nineteenth century (Scale 2/3).

sophisticated works of art.

Finally, the search for graffiti occupied parts of my summer holidays in Whitby during 1986, 1987 and 1988. Most of those worthy of recording were revealed by raking light of a flat-beam torch - the ideal type was found to be one of those with a fluorescent tube, which provides a flat even light over a relatively wide area. Only a few of the graffiti were visible to the unaided eye.

Having located them, I recorded the examples by placing a large sheet of thin paper over the area and rubbing evenly with a very soft black wax crayon. This produced a 'negative' image, the undisturbed surface of the pew showing up black and the graffiti as white lines upon it. Despite the great care taken, it is possible that some representations were missed.

Figure 12. North Transept, Newholm Pew, 2nd from Rear). Extremely faint but well-executed carving of a brigantine, apparently named *Lucy*, but too indistinct to be picked up on the rubbing. The drawing is enhanced with details taken from a photograph.

While some carvings were as clear and fresh as the day they were carved, others had been camouflaged by layers of varnish or by artificial wood-graining. One or two were visible to the eye but would not rub satisfactorily. In these instances I photographed them with a raking light and then used the two images to create a composite.

There is always some temptation, carefully avoided here, to improve upon or correct what appears in the graffiti. The only editorial control I have exercised has been that of removing from the transcriptions any line, mark or initial which does not seem to belong to the original. This is often difficult to judge because in places the graffiti overlie or intercut each other quite thickly. In cases of doubt I have erred on the side of leaving these marks. Errors are, of course, possible where the original is either very worn or faint, such as when it has been varnished over.[15]

Figure 13. North Transept, Rear Pew. A detailed but perhaps unfinished graffito of a paddle-steamer named at bow and stern *Emu*. Alone of all the carvings this one can be identified with a particular vessel. Built on the Tyne in 1871 of 73 tonnes, *Emu* was bought by the Whitby Steam-Tug Association and came to Whitby in 1873 where she was involved in ferrying sightseers out to the Channel Fleet on its visit in the following year. She also carried on a regular service to Scarborough in the 1880s and suffered the indignity of running aground in full view of the Spa in 1888.[16]

Notes and Referenes

1. Whellan, T *History and Topography of the City of York and the North Riding of Yorkshire*, 1859, p253. The latest general history of Whitby is my own work *A History of Whitby*, 1993.

2. Daysh, GHJ (Editor), *A Survey of Whitby and the Surrounding Area,* 1958, p59.

3. Jeffrey, Percy Shaw, *Whitby Lore and Legend,* 3rd Edn. 1953, p52.

4. Pevsner, N *The Buildings of England; Yorkshire, The North Riding,* 1966, p395.

5. ibid, p392-3.

6. Taylor, A Clifton, *Another Six English Towns,* 1984, p.48-52.

7. Keane, Reverend, quoted by R.T. Gaskin, *The Old Seaport of Whitby,* 1909, p.373.

8. Pritchard, V *English Medieval Graffiti,* 1967, p.122-5.

9. Some impressions of the significant role of Whitby ships and shipbuilding can be gained from DR MacGregor, *Merchant sailing Ships: Sovereignty of Sail 1775-1815,* 1985, p57-64 and R Weatherill, *The Ancient Port of Whitby and its Shipping,* 1908.

10. Walker, D M *Whitby Shipping,* (Revised Edn.), 1971, p9; Young, Rev George, *A History of Whitby,* 1817 (Reprinted 1976), p562-8.

11. Finch, R *Coals from Newcastle,* 1973, p75-6.

12. Whitby is most fortunate in possessing the similarly candid photographs of Frank Meadow Sutcliffe who worked in the late nineteenth- and early-twentieth centuries. They can be found most conveniently in the two volumes on Sutcliffe by W Eglon Shaw, 1974 and 1978, and later volumes by M Shaw.

13. Smith, G *King's Cutters; The Revenue Service and the War against Smuggling,* 1983, p.109-24.

14. Gaskin, 1909, p370.

15. An earlier and shorter version of this article appeared in *Folk Life,* 1990.

16. Godfrey, A *Pleasure Steamers of Old Yorkshire,* nd, p.22,27; White, 1993, p112.

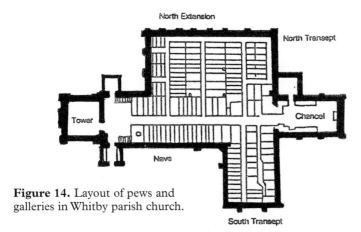

Figure 14. Layout of pews and galleries in Whitby parish church.

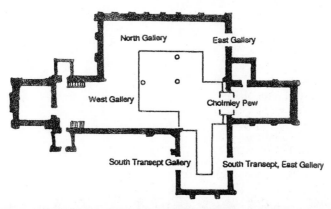

8. Happy Days – Images of Edwardian Filey

by Michael Fearon

MANY COMMUNITIES have a period in their history to which residents look back almost with a feeling of nostalgia, even if such a period was not part of their own experience. For Filey, this time was those few years between the end of the Boer War and the beginning of the First World War. That this is so, is confirmed by the enthusiasm with which Filonians have welcomed and supported in recent years the Edwardian Festival.

Why is this period so special in the minds of residents of Filey? Of several possible reasons two at least applied nationally. The Boer War caused so much distress that its end was welcomed with relief; and the years preceding the First World War were generally peaceful and have been looked back upon by people caught up in the tragedies of first one, then another World War as an almost halcyon period. Many view the time as one exhibiting a kind of innocence lost for ever in 1914. Secondly, contemporary photographs indicate that in terms of dress and fashion it was a time of elegance with very distinctive styles of apparel for both men and women.

By the 1890s, New Filey had established a 'fashionable' reputation. The distinction between Old Filey and New Filey was still a very real one, the dividing line being roughly along Murray Street. By this time the building of the Crescent (Figure 1) and adjacent

Figure 1. The Crescent, the premier street in Filey.

Figure 2. Crescent Gardens and early bandstand c.1905.

streets was complete; the Crescent Gardens (Figure 2) also were laid out and available for strolling in, particularly after Sunday morning church services. Filey's reputation as a resort 'free from all vulgarity' with good hotels, boarding houses and entertainment had become well established, and for a town of Filey's size the variety of shops was quite impressive.

One development that became apparent as Filey entered the twentieth century was the wider range of leisure activities that residents and visitors found available in the town. Music was the basis for many forms of entertainment provided by both amateur and professional performers and, on occasion, those associated with the London stage could be seen and heard in Filey. In July 1901, booked to appear at the Victoria Hall, were Miss Irene Moncrieff, Miss Edith Broad, Mr Llewellyn Cadwaladr and Mr H Carr-Evans, described as being from the Gaiety and Savoy Theatres, the D'Oyly Carte and Sir Augustus Harris Opera Companies. The Crescent Gardens Subscription Band was a very popular provider of light music during the season, usually playing both in the morning and evening.

The opening of the Grand Theatre on 15 February 1911 added a most important venue for a wide range of events. Not only was it designed to be both picture house and theatre, but it also had a tea room below the main entrance and a room suitable to be used either as a lecture or billiard room.

In August 1913 two special occasions were the performance of *The Quaker Girl* by George Dance's Company from the Adelphi Theatre, London, and from Daly's Theatre, Mr George Edwardes' Company in *The Merry Widow*. Rather less professional perhaps, were the two Italian organ grinders who in September 1900 were fined twelve shillings each for continuing to play after being ordered to cease! Seen also at the Grand in its earliest days were amateur productions such as *Pearl, The Fishermaiden* produced by the Filey Amateur Operatic Society.

The Visitors' Lists indicate how holiday patterns were changing as the Victorian era gave way to the Edwardian. To nineteenth century Filey came men and women for a change of scene, health-giving sea air, gentle exercise and a little socialising; in many cases their children remained at home. However, by the early years of this century the lists indicate that more children were now coming with their parents to the seaside accompanied by maids, nurses and governesses. Filey was now seen to be a resort for all the family.

By Edwardian times there was a greater variety of amusements and entertainments in Filey than ever before. In addition to the orchestra which played in the Crescent Gardens, the Pierrots performed on the beach or Foreshore, the Golf Club was well-established and there were opportunities for both residents and visitors to take part in Sports Days, Walking Matches or Hockey, Cricket and Football Matches. In 1906 a heated swimming pool, sixty feet by nineteen feet, was built at Primrose Valley, primarily for the pupils of Southcliffe School, but also available to others. There were also the Liberal and Conservative Clubs, a Gymnastic and Athletic Club, a Cycling Club, and a Choral Society; University Extension Lectures and occasional Fancy Dress balls. Between 1910 and 1912 there were also those daring young men in their flying machines performing astonishing aerial deeds from their base at Primrose Valley.

A major factor in the successful development of New Filey was John Wilkes Unett's decision to designate a substantial area as pleasure grounds which subsequently became known as the North and South Crescent Gardens (Figure 3). For many years these gardens were for the enjoyment only of the owners and occupiers of, and visitors to, the houses on and close to The Crescent; in a manner similar to that which pertains today in some London squares. Later, these gardens were made available to all and entertainments were put on for summer visitors.

As it was designed to do, the development of New Filey, coupled with the arrival of the railway, led to a very rapid increase in the number of visitors to the town. In days long before the creation of departments of tourism, television advertising and the printing and wide distribution of coloured brochures, it must have been very much by word of mouth and personal recommendation that Filey so rapidly became known the length and breadth of the country.

The middle years of the nineteenth century were also considerably previous to the days of holidays with pay, and thoughts of going away to stay at hotel or boarding-house were held almost exclusively only by those people of some substance. One significant difference between those and more recent times is in the comparative numbers who came from different parts of the country. Today we know that a high proportion of our visitors come from West and South Yorkshire, the Midlands and the North-East; however, a century ago the pattern was somewhat different. A much higher proportion came from London and the Home Counties with

Figure 3. Unett's plan for New Filey, 1835, showing the Crescent and Crescent Gardens.

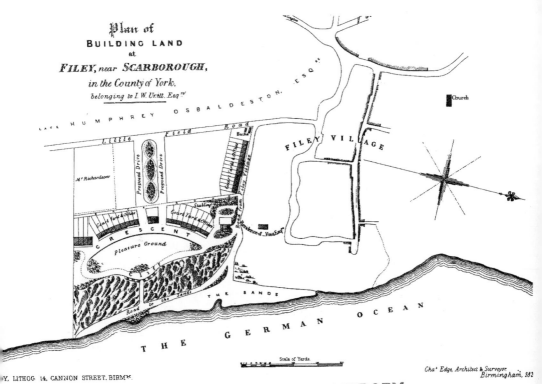

relatively few visitors from the then West Riding.

What is quite understandable is that Filey was an obvious choice as a seaside resort for those families of means who lived relatively close by. Thus, the names appearing in the visitors' lists week by week included the Earl of Feversham's family from Duncombe Park, Helmsley, staying with Mrs Barker, at 24 Crescent, in August 1873; Viscount Halifax and family from Pocklington, staying at 3 Belle Vue with Mrs Abbot late in the season in 1890, and Lord Londesborough at the *Foord's Hotel* in 1876. Sir Joseph and Lady Terry were frequent visitors in the 1890s, sometimes staying at *Langford Villa*; Lord and Lady Wenlock (Wenlock Place, Church Street, presumably has a nominal link with the family) of Escrick Park, York, chose the *Crescent Hotel* in 1878 for their holiday as did Viscount and Viscountess Folkestone, who, in spite of their name, had only to travel from Nun Appleton, Tadcaster, in September 1872. The Howards from Castle Howard spent part of the summer at 26 Crescent in 1887, and from Burton Agnes Hall, the Wickham-Boyntons took rooms with Mrs Webster on the Foreshore in the early years of this century. In the 1870s members of the Wombwell family of Newburgh Priory, near Coxwold, holidayed on the Crescent at Numbers 15 and 17. Also choosing the Crescent in Edwardian times were Lord and Lady Bolton, of Bolton Hall, Leyburn, who spent several weeks with Mrs Cunningham at Number 2 and Lord Deramore's family from Heslington Park, York, lodged with Miss Gibson at *Osborne House*. About the same time, at the same boarding house, Lord St Oswald's family came from Nostell Priory, near Wakefield, for a July holiday. The previous year they had found accommodation with Mrs Hall, at 3 Melville Terrace.

One of the most splendidly situated summer residences was *North*

Figure 4. North Cliff Villa, which was later converted into a convalescent home.

Cliff Villa (Figure 4), and it was chosen in 1890 by the family of Lord Lascelles. In 1878 the family of the Archbishop of York took the house for the season and the Archbishop joined them when clerical duties allowed.

Another well-known churchman to visit Filey was Dean Farrar, of Canterbury, who stayed at *Cliff Point Cottage*, home of Mrs Dunn, in September 1888. One family which had only a short distance to travel in 1908 was that of Viscount Ennismore, of Hackness Grange; Mrs Cunningham's boarding house at 2 Crescent, was their chosen holiday home. Lord and Lady Middleton had only a little further to travel to the *Crescent Hotel* from their home at Birdsall near Malton in October 1881; and Viscountess Helmsley, of Nawton Tower, would soon reach the *Crescent Hotel* in 1912 whether she chose to travel by road or rail.

For these visitors, Filey would be one of the closest resorts to their homes and a popular choice, particularly for those who wished to avoid much travelling. However, the town clearly had its attractions for those who lived further away. In the years 1904 and 1905, young members of the Duke of Devonshire's family were staying at Mrs Gibson's boarding house at 12 Crescent and in the closing months of the 1890s some of the Earl of Wharncliffe's family stayed at 37 Crescent. From Wentworth Woodhouse (reputed to be the largest private house in Britain), the Earl and Countess Fitzwilliam and members of their family came to stay on the Crescent over a period of several years choosing either the *Crescent Hotel*, 30 Crescent, or 2 South Cliff Villas. Viscount and Viscountess Mountgarret, of Nidd Hall, spent part of the summer of 1907 at the *Royal Crescent Hotel* and the following year their family stayed with Mrs Whitfield at *Glenavon* on the Foreshore. From Kettering in the years 1902, 1903 and 1904 the Earl and Countess of Dalkeith, or members of their family, travelled to Filey to stay at either 2 or 3 Belle Vue. A family which made several visits to the town between 1868 and 1888 was that of the Duke of St Albans, from Nottinghamshire. The Duke favoured the *Crescent Hotel,* but members of his family preferred either *North Cliff Villa* or Mrs Haxby's establishment at 17 Crescent. In 1908 the Marchioness of Exeter brought her family from Burghley House, Stamford, to stay with Mrs Barwick at 16 Crescent, but four years later she came alone to stay with Mrs Cunningham at 2 Crescent. Perhaps neighbours Lord and Lady Cecil recommended Filey following their holiday here at 11 Crescent in 1904 and 1905. A much earlier visitor from Stamford was Lord Kesteven who stayed at the *Crescent Hotel* in September 1878. Another Midlands visitor was Lord Byron (not the poet) who spent a holiday in August 1884 at the *Spa Saloon*. Also staying on the sea-front in August 1903, at *Pitfour* (now part of *Southdown*) were Viscount and Viscountess Combermere from Stafford. Regular visitors to Filey throughout the 1890s were family members of Viscount Newarks of Holme Pierrepoint. They usually boarded with Mrs Atkinson at 19 Crescent.

The attractions of Filey must have been discussed over many of London's dinner tables, for week by week and year by year many made the long railway journey between the Capital and Filey. Among these were, in 1874, Lord Loftus, and Baron and Baroness de Vaux and a little later, Viscountess Chewton (1878); also Viscount and Viscountess Tiverton (1908); Earl Waldegrave (1878); the Earl of Bessborough (1876); the Countess of Guilford (1908) and the Earl and Countess of Halsbury (1908). The *Crescent Hotel* was the most popular destination for the majority of these as it was also for many other London residents, such as the Duke and Duchess of Newcastle (1890) and the Dowager Duchess of Northumberland in 1905. From Grosvenor Square in July 1881 Lord De Freyne also came to the *Crescent Hotel* and in August 1871 Lady Hamilton enjoyed the hotel's hospitality. The previous year, the Duke of Grafton's son, Lord Frederick Fitzroy took the same route staying at both the hotel and 26 Crescent. In 1874, having a July seaside holiday at the *Crescent Hotel* were members of the Duke of Westminster's family and those of the Marquis of Ely. Wimbledon residents, the Earl and Countess of Chichester, had an autumn break in 1901. From Eaton Place to Varley's *Crescent Hotel* in September 1892, journeyed the Marquis of Ailesbury's son, Lord Brudenell Bruce and to the same hotel in July 1874, came Baron and Lady Amphlett and party from Wimpole Street, London. A later visit was made to the *Crescent Hotel* by Viscount Hood in September 1909.

Others from London and the Home Counties staying elsewhere in the town included the Earl and Countess of Verulam, boarding at 5 Unett Street *(Southdene)* in 1900; the family of Viscountess Chelsea enjoying Mrs Waggitt's hospitality at 28 Crescent; the Marchioness of Hastings from Windsor, staying with Mrs Bulmer on the Foreshore at *Arndale* (between *Swiss Villa* and *Matlock House*) in September 1906; in 1912 members of the Marquis of Zetland's family, also stayed on the front at Mrs Chapman's, *St Kitt's*; Lord and Lady Milnes Gaskill at Mrs Cunningham's, 2 Crescent in August 1907; and the Earl and Countess of Yarmouth stayed with Miss Preston at 27 Crescent. From St James's Palace to Mrs Proctor's boarding house at 31 Crescent in August 1907, came Lady Valda Machell, and to 15 Crescent in 1867 and two successive years came members of a family with a rather fine combination of title and address - Lord Portman of Portman Square.

More distant travellers to Filey were Lord and Lady Alington and family from Dorset. Their chosen holiday home in August 1884 was 8 Crescent. The Marchioness of Bath and family had a slightly shorter journey from Longleat to Mrs Gofton's at 2 Belle Vue in 1899 and 1901. To adjacent 3 Belle Vue in 1908 came the Duke and Duchess of Norfolk and family from Arundel Castle; the family came again in 1910 and 1912. From Shillinglee Park, Sussex, in 1879, journeyed the Wintertons; the Earl staying at the *Crescent Hotel*, and the Countess and family with Mrs Cullen at 15 Crescent. In August 1901, one of Mrs Atkinson's guests at 19 Crescent was Viscount Torrington, whose ancestor wrote *Rides Around Britain* under the name John Byng. He had travelled from Kent. Another, earlier visitor from Kent, was the Countess Stanhope who lodged with Mrs Ellis at 1 Belle Vue in September 1892.

The rather difficult journey from North Wales did not deter Lord and Lady Penrhyn and members of their family who came from Penrhyn Castle, Bangor, to Filey several times between the years 1887 and 1905 to stay either at *Downcliff*; the *Ackworth* (Figure 5), the *Crescent Hotel* or 3 Belle Vue; nor would Lord and Lady Decies have an easy journey from Windermere when they stayed at with Mrs Cullen at 15 Crescent in June 1872.

Relatively few visitors came to Filey from the north of England or Scotland. Among the few who did included the Countess of Desart in September 1871 who came from Hexham to the *Crescent Hotel*; the family of the Earl of Mar and Kellie who stayed, in August 1901, with Mrs Hall at 3 Melville Terrace; Lord and Lady Clive of Scothay

Figure 5. *Ackworth Hotel* and Promenade, Filey.

Castle, Lanark, who also chose the *Crescent Hotel* in 1871; the Earl of Northesk, staying at the *Royal Crescent Hotel* in August 1900 and the family of the Earl and Countess of Minto from Hawick who lodged with Mrs Railton at 2 Melville Terrace in July 1893.

A family which became very closely associated with the town over many years was that of the Earl and Countess of Ranfurly. They made the journey numerous times between Dungannon, in Ireland, and the resort during the years 1884 to 1907, putting up at either the *Crescent Hotel*, 2 and 3 Crescent or taking residence often at *Downcliff*. The Earl, who was appointed Governor-General of New Zealand in 1897, entered fully into Filey's social life, often acting as referee in sports and fishing competitions. Another visitor from Ireland was Lord Oxmantown who stayed here in July 1909 at 12 Crescent.

Filey also achieved an international reputation and a degree of distinction as a holiday resort with several members of the European aristocracy for whom the *Crescent Hotel* was a popular destination. These included, around the turn of the century, Count and Countess Telekei from Budapest; Count and Countess del Villar over from Madrid; Baron Massenbach and Baron and Baroness Von Shuralier of Darmstadt. Others staying about the same period were Baroness Van Langanan who came from Vienna to stay at *Wave Crest*; Count and Countess Kinsky lodging at 2 Belle Vue; Baroness de Chabonlan from Paris lodging with Miss Shaw at 2 Rutland Street and Baron Lauer of Berlin on holiday with his family at Miss Preston's boarding house at 27 Crescent.

In August 1879, the Count and Countess Karolyi took a break from diplomatic duties at the Austrian Embassy to enjoy the sea views from 16 Crescent. In 1909, Baroness Von Turbeuf preferred the more homely environment of 17 Church Street. One of Filey's very few Italian visitors was Baron Rondi who in July 1879, was almost in the countryside while staying at *Grove Villa* on the Scarborough Road. In August 1907 the *Crescent Hotel* entertained a guest from one of the most distant parts of the Empire in the person of the Ranie of Sarawak.

Filey was also popular with senior officers of the Army and Navy, from General Clarke, of London, in September 1877 on leave at the *Crescent Hotel*, to Rear Admiral Mosteyn Field staying with Miss Cappleman at *Beach Haven* in 1908. Other military men who found Filey a good place in which to enjoy a respite from duty included General Goddard, of London, staying with his family at Mrs Hepton's boarding house at 4 Rutland Terrace in September 1884;

General Gloag and family enjoying Mrs Scrivener's hospitality next door at number three at almost the same time; they perhaps recommended the establishment to General Cox, of Guildford, who took a summer break there in 1887.

The *Crescent Hotel* may have resembled a rather good officers' mess during one week in August 1890, when Colonels Goodchild, Beaumont, Collins and Pigott were staying there with their families. In 1896, General and Mrs Philips chose Mrs Atkinson's boarding house at 18 Crescent for their late summer break. Number 18 Crescent was also popular with the Church, for staying there at various times between 1868 and 1909 were the Lord Bishop of Lincoln and family; the Lord Bishop of Wakefield and the Dean of Chester and family.

The visitors' lists also record some intriguing names; who, for instance, were Mr and Mrs Roosevelt, of New York, who spent a few days at 10 Crescent in August 1902? And how pleased would be the visitor to the *Crescent Hotel* in August 1896 who was listed simply as 'Hon Trollop'? More familiar names are those of Sacheverell Sitwell, staying with his family at 18 Crescent in July 1874 and Mrs C F Wedgwood from Burlaston boarding at 15 Crescent in October 1871, undoubtedly of the famous pottery family; Mr and Mrs A Rowntree, of York, at 4 Parade (*Foreshore*) in July 1910 and another noted name in the chocolate world, Mr and Mrs Barrow Cadbury, of Birmingham, stayed at Mrs Hall's, 27 Crescent, in August 1908; Mr and Mrs Reckitt, Hessle, were at 11 Crescent in 1879; and Master Neville Chamberlain was at Mrs Brown's, Belle Vue, in August 1881. Who was in the party brought for the season by the splendidly named Madame Risk Allah to *Rose Cottage*, Mitford Street, in 1876? In September 1905, a guest of Mrs Cammish at 6 Crescent, was the particularly well-known Yorkshireman the Hon F S Jackson, the County cricket team captain.

Another notable family to visit Filey was that of Titus Salt, the enlightened textile manufacturer who built the complex of mills together with the new town of Saltaire in the West Riding. In August 1871 he stayed at the *Crescent Hotel*, while his son, also named Titus and family chose Mrs Perryman's boarding house at 23 Crescent. In order to enjoy a break from civic duties in August 1910, the Lord Mayor and Lady Mayoress of London took up residence at the *Royal Crescent Hotel*.

A young visitor to the town who later achieved international fame in the world of music was Frederick Delius. Born at Bradford in January 1862, his father was a wool merchant who brought his family to Filey many times between the years 1876 and 1901. It was their practice to journey here from Bradford in a special carriage attached to a scheduled train. In later years, Delius recalled with pleasure playing cricket at Gristhorpe and Hunmanby and spoke of a walk he took on the Brigg during which he was trapped by the tide. On 19 August 1879, while staying at Mrs Colley's, 5 Crescent, Delius played two violin solos, *Cavatina* by Raff and *Sonata* by Grieg, during a musical evening - perhaps one of the first occasions on which he played in public. Interestingly, he could not possibly have anticipated that just seven years later he would number Grieg as a friend while studying music in Leipzig. Other houses at which the family stayed included 22 and 24 Crescent, *Ivydale* and *Worlaby House* in Rutland Street.

Another visitor who later became equally celebrated, but in the world of letters, was Charlotte Bronte (Figure 6), author of *Jane Eyre*. She came to Filey in June 1849 after attending her sister's death in Scarborough. Charlotte stayed for three weeks with her life-long friend, Ellen Nussey, at *Cliff House* (now the Bronte Cafe) in Belle Vue Street. Clearly she benefitted by her sojourn for she returned in May 1852 to stay for a month again at *Cliff House*; this time she was alone, and to pass the time frequently walked on the beach and once bathed in the sea, at that time a novel experience. In a letter to Ellen Nussey she wrote '...I set out with intent to trudge to Filey Bridge [Brigg], but was frightened back by two cows. I mean to try again some morning.'

The *Filey Post* stopped publishing lists of visitors in 1915 and ceased publication altogether three years later. When the 'Great War' of 1914-18 ended, England had changed so markedly in just a few years that it is unlikely that visitors would have been listed again even if the *Post* had continued publication. It perhaps seems strange to us today that readers apparently preferred to peruse long lists of visitors names rather than read items of local, national or international news. Yet so it was, and such lists were not just confined to Filey, the *Scarborough Gazette*, in high season, also contained several large pages of visitors' lists as did the *Whitby Gazette*; but these lists do, however, enable us today to obtain a picture of the type of holidaymaker at Filey in those far-off Victorian and Edwardian days.

In addition to visits by the gentry, Filey was also popular with Royalty. Possibly the first royal visit was that

Figure 6. A portrait of Charlotte Bronte who enjoyed two holidays at Filey in the nineteenth century.

made by Leopold II, King of the Belgians. It took place in mid-September 1873 during the King's voyage to Scotland to stay with Queen Victoria at Holyroodhouse. At short notice he apparently decided to stay briefly in Scarborough for a private visit during which, in company with the Count D'Outremont, they drove over to Filey, alighting at the Crescent Hotel. From here they walked through the gardens and along the sands to the Brigg. Clearly it was a fine, early autumn day, for on their return they sat in front of the Spa Saloon for almost an hour to enjoy the view. They then returned to the *Crescent Hotel* just three hours late for luncheon which had been ordered for two o'clock!

A rather more prompt arrival for lunch at the same hotel was made seven years later by the Duke of Edinburgh, Queen Victoria's second son, known affectionately as the 'Sailor Prince'. This was during the official visit by the Duke in his capacity as Admiral-Superintendent of Naval Reserves. He drove over in a coach and pair from Scarborough, accompanied by Commander Grant, the Superintendent of Naval Reserves for the Scarborough District, in order to inspect the Coastguard Station which then was at the seaward end of Queen Street. Here the Duke of Edinburgh was greeted by a crowd of two hundred including the several local coastguards in full uniform and fishermen in guernseys and sou'westers. After the inspection he was shown plans recently drawn up for a harbour scheme at Filey, and then, following lunch, he left the town in a special saloon carriage attached to the midday Hull train en route for another coastguard station inspection at Flamborough.

Almost ten years later the Duke of Edinburgh's nephew also enjoyed the hospitality of the same establishment. In August 1890, Prince Albert Victor, the elder son of Prince Edward (later King Edward VII) drove from Scarborough in company with the Earl of Londesborough and Sir Charles Legard for a brief visit which included tea at the *Crescent Hotel.*

Another of Queen Victoria's large family to visit Filey was Princess Louise, the Queen's fourth daughter. She came over for a day from Harrogate in September 1899 with Lord and Lady Verulam who had holidayed here, and in the afternoon the Princess spent half an hour shopping in the town.

Perhaps it was she who recommended the resort to her niece Victoria, Queen Victoria's grand-daughter, for in the year 1900, Victoria and her husband, Prince Louis of Battenberg, stayed for several weeks at 36 Crescent with their children.

The Prince and Princess's off-spring were - Alice (to become mother of the Duke of Edinburgh); Louisa (later Queen of Sweden); George (later 2nd Marquess of Milford Haven) and Louis (later Earl Mountbatten). For the Prince, the time spent at Filey was a combination of business and pleasure. He was then Chief of the Naval Intelligence Department (he later became First Sea Lord of the Admiralty) and spent much of his days in local cobles investigating currents and tides. Louis, who was then just a few weeks old, contracted a childish ailment for which a remedy was supplied by local chemist W Rickard. Clearly the medicine proved acceptable since, for several years afterwards, Mr Rickard's advertisements carried the legend 'Under the Patronage of Her Grand Ducal Highness, Princess Louis of Battenberg, Princess of Hesse'.

In June 1910, again perhaps the result of a family recommendation, Queen Victoria's grandson, Ernest Ludwig (the Grand Duke of Hesse) stayed at the *Crescent Hotel* with his wife Eleanore and children George and Louis. Ernest's younger sister, Alix, Tsarina of Russia, was assassinated in 1918.

A popular visitor to Filey in the 1930s was Princess Mary, the Princess Royal and daughter of King George V, who brought her sons George, later Earl of Harewood, and Gerald. The boys enjoyed early morning fishing trips with Thomas 'Tich' Jenkinson, who provided them with an alarm clock with the recommendation that they should place it in a bucket in order to be ready to sail soon after dawn. The link was resumed in July 1955 when the Princess Royal presented Mr Jenkinson with the British Empire Medal (BEM) for services to the fishing industry. The presentation took place in the open air when the Princess Royal was in Filey to open officially the Royal Parade.

In the following year, on 16 May 1956, Countess Mountbatten in her capacity as Superintendent-in-Chief of the St John's Ambulance Brigade, opened the local Divisional Headquarters of that organisation in Mitford Street.

With the increase in visitor numbers, and the resort often under royal patronage, the question of suitable entertainments arose. In the closing years of the nineteenth century, visitors to the seaside everywhere were beginning to expect entertainment of a rather less serious nature than the small orchestras and bands that had previously been the most usual musical providers. Around the coast there were in the 1880s many troupes of Minstrels, but by the 1890s they were being replaced by the Pierrots in their equally distinctive costumes.

An early Pierrot around these parts - and one of the greatest showmen of the day, was Will Catlin (Figure 7), who first appeared at Scarborough in 1894 and eventually went on to develop the Futurist and Arcadia leisure complexes there. One of the performing Pierrots in Catlin's Bridlington company was Ernest Taylor who adopted the stage name Andie Caine. He came to Filey in 1895 and recognised that it was a resort in which he might establish his own troupe. Andie sang and played the banjo accompanied by George Fisher. Initially the pair found it hard going and spent many nights sleeping on the beach as the takings from their 'bottling' were insufficient to pay for lodgings.

Local reception to the performances of Pierrots was often less than cordial and sometimes hostile. In August 1899 five Pierrots, Teddy Myles, Charles Horner, Harry Collins, Edward Bleasdale and his brother Tommy were fined forty shillings for performing on the Crescent. Tommy Bleasdale was unusual as a Pierrot in that his chosen musical instrument was a harp, and one wonders if this perhaps gave inspiration to a later musical comic - Harpo Marx of

Figure 7. Will Catlin (centre) and his troupe of Pierrots.

the Marx brothers?

However, by this date, Andie Caine's little band was becoming accepted and the performers were described as 'Royal Filey Pierrots' because, on occasion, members of the Battenberg family were seen in the audience. Pierrots were becoming respectable; and so began Andie Caine's association with Filey which was to last for forty-six years until his death in 1941.

Not every visitor welcomed the Pierrots; in 1903 the local Council received a complaint that 'the town was being overrun by pierrots', that 'Filey was rapidly being brought down to the level of Margate and Yarmouth and that though Filey had been a haven of rest for the weary it was now like a moving, troubled sea.' These views were, however, held only by a small minority and Andie Caine's Pierrots established over many years great affection amongst residents and visitors. Children especially would come to know many of the comic pantomime routines by heart, but still ask for them to be repeated, and their appearance, season by season, was eagerly anticipated by returning visitors. One such performer who enjoyed substantial acclaim was the comedian Teddy Myles, who was described in 1903 as being 'in his eighth consecutive season, as light and clever and entertaining as heretofore'. Other later popular members of Caine's troupe were Carl Edwards - vocalist and entertainer, Fred Musson - comedian, Gus Yelrob and Billy Gill.

For many years the Royal Filey Pierrots became essential viewing for almost every visitor to the resort and Andie Caine became a respected and well-liked resident whose business interests, like Will Catlin's of Scarborough, were to expand and diversify and came to include the Grand Cinema. He was also responsible for staging London pantomimes, and in 1910 these included *Cinderella* at the Palace Theatre, Walthamstow, and *Red Riding Hood* at the Palace Theatre, Tottenham.

Figure 8. Pierrots performing on Scarborough beach around 1920. From the collection of Alan Whitworth.

The Pierrots performed during the day on the beach or the Foreshore, and in later years, at the Alfresco Pavilion behind the *Royal Crescent Hotel* on a site now occupied by the recently built *Newton Court*.

The hearing at Bridlington Police Court in 1906 when Andie Caine applied for a music licence for the Pavilion must have been nearly as enjoyable as a Pierrot performance, for his demeanour was described as 'entertaining alike to bench, bar and the police'. It became something of a tradition for guests at the *Crescent Hotel* to stroll over to the Pavilion in evening dress after dinner and round off the day with an hour or more of music and laughter.

Another Pierrot who came to and stayed in Filey was Lister Reekie. In his earlier days as an entertainer he had busked on Brighton Beach with Tom Walls who later made a very successful career in the theatre and in films and also achieved fame as the owner of a Derby winner *April the Fifth*. On joining the Filey troupe in 1913, Lister Reekie was known as Cousin Punch; in the following year his benefit performance unfortunately coincided with the outbreak of World War I and the consequent exodus of visitors from Filey. Interestingly, in 1931, he made an unexpected career change and established the *Filey News*, the resorts first local newspaper for many years.

Between the two World Wars Pierrots continued to perform, and indeed, after World War II, they performed again in Filey on the beach and sea front, but somehow the magic had gone along with those halcyon days which their style of entertainment evoked; perhaps with the increased popularity of the radio and gramophone audiences had become a little too sophisticated? Whatever the reason, however, Pierrots were a little later no more to be seen in the resort and an era of more than fifty years of popular light entertainment drew to a close.

Finally, no story of the holiday industry in Filey would be complete without reference to Butlin's Holiday Camp. The association with Butlin's Ltd and the town extended from 1939 over a period of forty-four years and during that time the presence of the Holiday Camp had a considerable effect on the town.

The first definite indication that William 'Billy' Butlin was interested in building a Camp close to Filey came in April 1939 on the eve of the second World War, when plans were submitted for approval to Filey Urban District Council. However, after discussion, these were rejected on the grounds that such a development would represent 'a serious detriment to the neighbourhood' and that the buildings were 'out of keeping with the locality.' This response resulted in several changes being made to the scheme of things and a special meeting being arranged between the Council members, Mr Butlin and the Manager of the Butlin's Holiday Camp at Clacton-on-Sea. That the changes were clearly satisfactory became apparent when in May of that year the amended plans were approved.

Work on the site began soon after, but just a few weeks later war broke out and a holiday by the sea was soon to be the last thing on people's minds. Notwithstanding, such a development of property, even in an unfinished state was not without use, and it was offered to the War Department for military accommodation. Hore Belisha then asked Billy Butlin what he would charge to complete the camp and was given an estimate of £175 per occupant. This figure Butlin knew to be seventy-five pounds less than the sum usually accepted by the War Department, but he coupled it with one condition; that at the end of the war he would be able to buy back the camp at a price of £105 per unit of accommodation. This arrangement was readily accepted.

Interestingly, one of the first major items to arrive on the newly acquired site was the fountain from the Glasgow Exhibition which was delivered in September 1939. When eventually it was assembled in the boating lake, it produced a circular pattern of illuminated water jets, and particularly on late summer evenings provided an impressive spectacle for campers leaving theatres and bars; before that though the initial function of the boating lake site was as a parade ground. When the camp reverted to its peacetime role, however, some difficulty was experienced in satisfactorily submerging the slightly inclined parade ground; a situation which led to the often heard comment among holiday-makers that 'the tide's still out at Butlin's.'

In the early summer of 1945 half the Camp was released by the War Department, and the first visitors began to arrive. The transition from war-time service station to peacetime Holiday Camp was eased by the appointment of Group Captain Ernest Borthwick-Clarke as the first Camp-Controller by Billy Butlin. This new position required no change in place of employment for Mr Borthwick-Clarke, as he was previously Officer Commanding RAF Hunmanby Moor, the name given to the camp as a service station.

After six years of war, campers came determined to have a memorable time and for many it was their first holiday away from home. To us today, their willingness to be organised into processions and group activities including physical training perhaps seems strange, but it was possibly due to the training received in the services which many had only just left.

In order to quickly establish the name and reputation of the Filey Holiday Camp, Billy Butlin arranged, in the Viennese ballroom, a week of grand opera beginning on 21 October 1946 with a performance of *La Boheme* by the San Carlo Opera Company of Naples. The company, which came direct from the Covent Garden Opera House, London, also presented later in the week *The Barber of Seville, Cavalleria Rusticana* and *Il Pagliacci*. The following year, on 10 May, to celebrate the opening that day of the Railway Station by the Lord Lieutenant of the East Riding, Lord Middleton, and Sir Charles Newton, Chief General Manager of the London North Eastern Railway company, a concert was given in the Viennese Ballroom. The soloist in Beethoven's *Piano Concerto No.3* was Solomon accompanied by the London International Orchestra conducted by Anatole Fistoulari. These occasions were open to local residents, a much appreciated gesture.

In those early post-war years holiday seasons were long; in 1947 the Camp opened on 29 March and the last campers of the season departed on 1 November that year.

In the succeeding years the Camp grew in size and in the range of facilities offered. In the late-1950s at the height of the season ten thousand campers and 1500 staff would be together creating a holiday atmosphere which many found irresistible and to which they would return season by season. On arrival, each camper was presented with an enamel lapel badge indicating the year and the Camp; some acquired a considerable collection of badges and wore as many as their lapels would hold.

Until self-catering facilities were offered in the late 1960s, all accommodation was in chalets of simple provision, and full-board was available in the four dining halls patriotically named Kent, Gloucester, Windsor and York. Each camper was assigned to one of these and thus became a member of a House of that name. The intensity of the inter-house rivalry that was generated in games and competitions and exhibited by campers in their new found loyalties would supply a sociologist with material for a lengthy thesis! Children were particularly well catered for and evening chalet patrols allowed parents to enjoy an evenings entertainment during which they would glance occasionally at an illuminated sign indicating where babies had been heard crying. The television series *Hi-de-Hi* conveyed well the atmosphere of the camp.

Several well-known entertainers began their careers at Filey; in the mid-1950s Charlie Drake was a boxing instructor and Des O'Connor, as a red-coat, did an excellent ad-lib act on Saturday morning's in the open air, sometimes in the rain, selling the Butlin's *Church Review* to campers waiting for coaches to take them home. A star by any standards was 'Big Charlie', a male Indian elephant weighing an estimated eight tons. Transporting him from his original home in Ayr, Scotland, to the camp at Filey had been a major engineering challenge. He walked frequently round the Holiday Camp and was very popular with the visitors. Sadly, when his mahout or handler died, he became difficult to handle and eventually had to be put down due to his unpredictable temperament.

Later, changing holiday patterns brought about the introduction of self-catering facilities and campers also began to indicate their increasing preference for less formal entertainments and management-style. Much later, continued changes and the introduction of cheap 'Package Holidays' brought about a decline in the Holiday Camp industry which led in time to the closure of many camps.

Although there had been indications in the early-1980s that all was not well with the Camp, it nevertheless came as a considerable shock to the staff and to the town when in late 1983 it was announced that the Filey Holiday Camp was to close completely. In the thirty-nine seasons of the Camp's life, a considerable number of jobs, both permanent and temporary, full and part-time had been taken by local people and would be sorely missed.

The average number of campers staying each season was in the order of a hundred thousand and most of these visited the town itself at least once during their holiday bringing much appreciated revenue. The many donations to local charitable causes made by Sir 'Billy' Butlin personally, or by the Camp staff, were always much appreciated. So ended an era, the permanent staff dispersed and local communities adjusted to the knowledge that no more would the Holiday Camp spring back into life with the beginning of another holiday season.

Today, despite changing patterns in the holiday season, Filey still remains dear to the hearts of many; and while day trippers come and go in season, taking away pleasant memories, yet there are still a great number who stay on for a traditional week or fortnight's rest and recreation in the grand manner of those Edwardian days, leaving refreshed and invigorated, ready to face anew the rigours of their daily lives.

9. Dovecotes and Pigeon-lofts of the East Coast

by Reg Brunton

SINCE ANCIENT TIMES man has kept pigeons in captivity, breeding and rearing them for their eggs, manure and for food. Possibly the Chinese were the first to domesticate the wild Rock Pigeon *(Columbia Livia)* from which all pigeon breeds are descended. Certainly on a ceramic model of a farmyard dating from 1000BC, dovecotes can clearly be seen on the house roof. However, it is from the Egyptians that we first learn of the 'art' of rearing pigeons - in particular, the farmers prized the pigeon dung which they liberally spread on their arid fields. The Persians from the same period in history utilised the pigeon droppings in the manufacture of gunpowder. Indeed, pigeon dung has been used variously in many commodities from medicines to aphrodisiacs!

On the subject of the introduction of pigeons into Britain little is known. Although pigeon rearing was practised by the Romans from a very early date as attested by many references in the 'classics', notably those written by Pliny, Varro and Columella, few 'columbaria' (pigeon houses) were established in England and the industry does not appear to have been of any importance in Britain until the time of the crusades when returning pilgrims and knights brought back many useful notions picked up during their journeys through the lands of the Saracens.

Historically, it is thought it is to the Normans that England owes a debt for the establishment of the large architectural pigeon house or dovecote into the landscape of the country.

France had long had a history of dovecotes, possibly inherited from its occupation by the Romans, and following the 'conquest' of Britain, the Norman lords brought to our shores their culture and manorial system with its feudal rights - and foremost among the privileges which these twin dominants, lord and clergy, aggregated to themselves, was that of being the sole classes of persons to build great pigeon houses wherein the birds of these favoured few might live, board free, at the expense of industrious crop-raising tenant neighbours - a factor which contributed in France in later centuries, to the onset of the French Revolution.

Early dovecotes are massive, round and were usually associated with monastic or manorial origins. Often they were architecturally crude with little decoration, small plain doorways, with few openings for light and air, but as architectural styles developed, and the laws of who could own a pigeon house changed in the seventeenth century, their construction and purpose altered and they became more flamboyant in design. Eventually the craze of pigeon rearing attained such proportions that by the eighteenth century it is said over 26,000 dovecotes existed in England alone! However, with changes in agricultural practises the need for killing off the livestock in winter disappeared and along with this change, the need for fresh pigeon meat as a food supplement - and the dovecote declined in importance, only briefly seeing an emergence in the early nineteenth century when 'gentlemen' required large numbers of birds for shooting purposes.

On the East Coast, the near proximity of the sea meant fish was possibly the staple diet for many, however, not a few dovecotes and pigeon-lofts existed from ancient times, some of which have survived to this day.

Probably the oldest remaining is the beautifully restored dovecote at *Low Hall*, Brompton-by-Sawden (Figure 1) not far from Scarborough along the A170. Dating from around the year 1400, it is little altered from its original form and pre-dates the present hall which was demolished and rebuilt in the 1640s, when during that period, the dovecote gables were altered to their present stepped-gabled design (Figure 2) and a mullion window inserted in the southern elevation while an elaborate perch and glover was placed centrally across the roof ridge, which has since been removed, possibly during the mid-nineteenth century when the roof was stripped, related and the medieval roof tiles replaced.

Measuring approximately 7m x 6m, the dovecote has a steeply pitched roof. The walls, 1.5m thick, are constructed of rough limestone blocks set in clay. Internally, the 6m high side walls and 8m gable ends are lined with over 1000 nest boxes starting one metre from the ground. These L-shaped boxes are built into the thickness of the walls, turning

Figure 1. Low Hall, Brompton-by-Sawden. Posibly the oldest surviving dovecote in the Scarborough district. *Photograph Alan Whitworth, courtesy Yorkshire Dovecote Society*

left and right on alternate rows, and each row having an alighting ledge projecting slightly forward of the main wall. The nest holes themselves measure 60cm deep with entrances about 20cm square.[1]

Externally, the corner quoins, string course and carved projecting rat ledge just below the eaves and extending round the gables, are of Hackness stone which has not weathered well, and seems to be re-used material from an earlier building.[2]

The roof structure is of oak with massive purlins and wall plates, to which are pegged oak rafters. Originally there were no braces, but when the roof was strengthened in the seventeenth century to take the stone slabs of the roof glover, they were added. Significantly, there has never been a ridge board.

The timberwork is covered with stone roofing tiles, each with a central hole near to the top edge through which was driven an oak peg to hang the tile over the laths fixed to the rafters. In order to give an impression of greater height, the

Figure 2. Low Hall, Brompton-by-Sawden. Detail of the stepped-gable showing the three original access holes (now blocked) and the remaining curious alighting ledges around the large window. *Photograph Alan Whitworth, courtesy Yorkshire Dovecote Society*

lower courses were of larger stones up to 60cm x 75cm, gradually decreasing toward the ridge where they measured only about 12cm x 15cm. In all, 850 tiles cover each side. The tiles, which would have required considerable labour to manufacture and perforate, are of Oolitic limestone which slits readily into then slabs and was quarried in the Forge Valley, some six miles to the east of the hall.

In 1974 *Low Hall* was purchased and a programme of restoration was undertaken under the guidance of architect Peter G Farmer, which included work on the pigeon house, by then, in a state of disrepair, particularly the roof in which there was a large hole in one side where the lathes had rotted away and the tiles slipped. Elsewhere, areas had been patched with slates and pantiles, and extensive surface pointing had been employed to fix loose tiles, some of which were wired onto the timberwork. In places, non-local stone had been used in repairs and tiles of the wrong size fitted into gaps.

Because of this piecemeal patching, the entire roof was stripped and the oak timbers treated. Lathes were replaced and the whole roof was retiled using as much as was preservable of the medieval tiling. Old oak pegs were removed and new fitted. Altogether some five and a quarter tonnes of stone was replaced on each side of the roof before rebedding and pointing the tops of the gables and ridge, and patching up the worst areas of the external stonework. Finally, a new weathervane in the form of a pigeon was made and fitted to the existing mounting.[3]

Today, the dovecote sits in magnificent isolation in the centre of a small paddock as it did when first put up. Rectangular in plan it has a well-fashioned central low-arched doorway and dressed windows with chamfered reveals.

In later centuries a number of other dovecotes are mentioned as existing at Brompton. The former *Buck Inn* possessed a dovecote, documented between 1762 and 1782.[4] Another stood in Hungate in 1774 and 1777 and probably belonged to the Cayley family,[5] and a further dovecote at 'Sawden' [Brompton] is mentioned in the will of Richard Casse, yeoman, dated 1744.[6]

Elsewhere, another early pigeon house is that stood beside *Cloughton Hall* (Figure 3), on the road between Scarborough and Whitby. This is of undetermined age and is of a type known as 'beehive' dovecotes and represents one of the earliest types of dovecotes built. Such beehive dovecotes which survive are more commonly found in the north of the county around the valley of the river Tees, where about half-a-dozen still stand from the thirteenth and fourteenth centuries. Other beehive dovecotes can be found dotted around the highlands of Scotland, where it is probable that this type of pigeon house originated and in the wilds of Cornwall. The beehive dovecote at *Cloughton Hall* is the furthest south in this county that I have found such a dovecote.

Slightly different from the traditional beehive pigeon house it

Figure 3. Cloughton Hall. A variation on the 'beehive' dovecote, the most ancient form of pigeon house in existence. Here we see a three tiered example. *Photograph Alan Whitworth, courtesy Yorkshire Dovecote Society.*

is round in plan, as they all are, constructed of rough coursed rubblestone but differs in being built in three tiers marked with set-offs before the domed roof of stone slabs is formed. The roof is surmounted today with a wooden glover or lantern, undoubtedly put on at a later date, as in all other instances, the roof was left with a central hole protected with a stone slab on short stumps which allowed access for the birds to fly in and out while keeping out the weather.

At Hackness, dovecotes have stood since the fourteenth century when a pigeon house was mentioned as early as 1301, which may have been the same listed in the Rent Rolls of Whitby Abbey in 1395, worth 12d.[7] The site of this dovecote is not known, but c.1550, a 'dovecote for 100 pairs of doves' belonged to the *Manor House* of Hackness, which may have been the same building as the double dovehouse or 'coate' mentioned in 1690 and 1696[8] which was pulled down in 1798 because it obscured the view from the new Hall.[9]

Figure 4. Keeper's Cottage, Hackness. A square two-storey dovecote in a cottage garden, and unusual in having a vaulted roof to the ground floor ceiling. Photograph Alan Whitworth, courtesy Yorkshire Dovecote Society

Today, only one dovecote remains at Hackness, stood in the garden of Keeper's Cottage (Figure 4), over-looking the present *Hackness Grange*. This dates from the mid- to late-eighteenth century.

Built of dressed sandstone with a pyramidal slate roof, it is square on plan and stands two stories high. Around the building at first floor level is a raised band or rat ledge to deter rodents from scaling the wall and gaining access to the interior. In the upper storey is a round window to the front with a single semi-circular or lunette window on the east and west elevations in a tooled stone surround. The ground floor has, unusually, a stone tunnel-vault roof with a trap-door giving access to the upper storey which is lined with brick nest boxes in all four walls.

Of a similar date is the early-eighteenth century hexagonal red

Figure 5. Reighton Hall. A beautiful hexagonal brick dovecote with nest boxes inside. *Photograph Alan Whitworth, courtesy Yorkshire Dovecote Society*

brick dovecote in Flemish bond stood to the rear of *Reighton Hall* (Figure 5), six miles south of Filey on the A165. Again, two stories high, it has a pantile roof and segmental arched windows of gauged brick and modillion eaves to the pointed roof. Inside, all the walls are lined floor to ceiling with L-shaped nest boxes which turn left and right on alternate rows.

Another early-eighteenth century pigeon houses stands just east of West Flotmanby Farmhouse at Folkton. Built of red brick in garden wall bond, it has sandstone quoins to the four corners and a pantile roof which retains a timber glover or lantern which allows access for the birds. The roof eaves are coved. Two stories high, unfortunately, inside, the nest boxes with ledges only survive in two walls.

At Filey, north of *Church Cliffe House* [Farm], which stands east of Filey parish church, is one of the largest dovecotes on the coast (Figure 6). Square in plan and two-storey in height, it is constructed of coursed rubble limestone standing on a plinth and surmounted by a squat, hipped roof. Encircled by a rat ledge at first floor level in the shape of a chamfered band, there are few openings, an original small low square-headed doorway in the west side with chamfered lintel and chamfered, irregular quoined jambs and a later horizontal, slit-like opening with a wooden alighting ledge beneath facing south into the garden which allows access birds

Figure 6. Church Cliffe House, Filey. One of the largest dovecotes on the coast. *Photograph Alan Whitworth, courtesy Yorkshire Dovecote Society*

access to the interior in which all four walls are lined from floor to ceiling with nest boxes and ledges. The building dates from the late-seventeenth or early-eighteenth century, and was probably re-roofed in the nineteenth century.

Near to Whitby, at *Ewe Cote Hall,* Ewe Cote, a tiny hamlet on the outskirts of the town, a dovecote of locally-quarried stone and of possible eighteenth century date can be found. Rectangular in plan with a ridged pantile roof with stone kneelers, the dovecote is two storeys high and has a window in the gable end with three small access holes above in the gable apex for the ingress of the birds.

Again, like Hackness and Brompton, in previous centuries dovecotes were quite common around Whitby, and one is mentioned as standing at Newholm, where in 1539-40, John Hexham paid rents amounting to 79s 8d to the abbey of St Hilda at Whitby for the lease of a 'farm ...with dovecote, orchards and gardens.'[10] Indeed, the abbey of St Hilda itself had a dovecote during the same period which stood in the Infirmary Garth and which was let to Sir Richard Cholmley for twenty-one years after the dissolution of the monastery.[11]

While in the neighbourhood of Whitby, perhaps one of the most curious dovecotes surviving is that stood like a chimney pot on the roof of a former coach house at Aislaby (Figure 7). Probably of eighteenth century date, this pigeon house comprises of a tall cylindrical column

Figure 7. Aislaby (near Whitby), Coach House. A most unusual nesting arrangement high on the roof of a former coach house. *Photograph Alan Whitworth, Yorkshire Dovecote Society*

Figure 8. Ivy House Farm, Aislaby (near Whitby). A traditional dovecote, possibly dating from the eighteenth century, now converted to a house. *Photograph Alan Whitworth, courtesy Yorkshire Dovecote Society*

Figure 9. Little Bella Farm, Flixton. Almost a ruin, it possibly pre-dates the farmhouse (behind). *Photograph Alan Whitworth, courtesy Yorkshire Dovecote Society*

Figure 10. North Street, Hunmanby. A roofles ruin; this shows the nineteenth century repairs i brick. *Photograph Alan Whitworth, courtesy Yorkshire Dovecote Socie*

Figure 11. North Street, Hunmanby. Detail of the original chalk stone nest boxes. *Photograph Alan Whitworth, courtesy Yorkshire Dovecote Society*

Figure 12. Bridlington Street, Hunmanby. Date 1897 - the year of Queen Victoria's Diamon Jubilee. *Photograph Alan Whitworth, courtesy Yorkshire Dovecote Socie*

of dressed stone with a domed top approximately six feet high by two feet in diameter with holes set all around in tiers with moulded stone banding between. This novel arrangement is home to perhaps two dozen birds. Across the road, in the yard of *Ivy House Farm* a second more traditionally recognisable square stone dovecote survives from the late-eighteenth century (Figure 8).

At *Little Bella Farm*, Flixton (Figure 9), a dovecote of eighteenth century date stands in a dilapidated condition. Constructed of rough coursed chalk blocks, it is rectangular in plan and has a ridged pantile roof. Inside, nest holes are built into the walls, although many are now blocked up. The dovecote stands in the paddock of a farm and appears older that the present farmhouse.

Another dovecote which is part ruinous and without roof is situated within the curtilage of No.10 North Street, Hunmanby (Figure 10). Here, again, the rectangular building to the rear of the property is built of rough coursed chalk blocks, but two walls have been repaired in previous centuries in red brick into which neat tiers of L-shaped nest boxes with alighting ledges turn left and right on alternate rows, while in the chalk stone walling a number of larger irregular nest boxes still survive (Figure 11).

A second dovecote can be found at Hunmanby (Figure 12). This is dated 1897 and was possibly erected to commemorate the Diamond Jubilee of Queen Victoria's reign. Rectangular, built of machine-made brick, it stands to the rear of a property on Bridlington Street and has a slate ridge-roof with wooden barge-boards to the gable ends.

Nineteenth century pigeon houses are less common in this area, and the majority hereabouts date from the eighteenth century. At present I know of only a handful, and the most spectacular of these is the one behind *Larpool Hall* (Figure 13), an eighteenth century mansion near Whitby, which, along with the adjoining stable block, has been converted into a house.

The dovecote is constructed of sandstone, is two-storey in height and has a hipped slate tiled roof. An exterior stone staircase at the rear gave access to the upper chamber in which the pigeons lived. Unfortunately, during conversion,

Figure 13. Larpool Hall, Whitby. A nineteenth century dovecote possibly incorporating carved stones from another building; shown during conversion to a house. *Photograph Alan Whitworth, courtesy Yorkshire Dovecote Society*

this was removed. The main facade, however, is little altered and has a pattern of holes and is decorated with blind arcading formed of carved square pillars on moulded bases and having foliated capitals. These appear to be re-used material from a demolished chapel and incorporated into this late-nineteenth century dovecote.

Another nineteenth century example, is the small pigeon loft formed in the roof of a nineteenth century single storey stable or coach house at *Court Green,* Cloughton which was formerly known as *Green Court* and was the 'home farm' to nearby *Cober Hill,* residence of Lord Airedale, newspaper proprietor. It is dated 1859 and three small pigeon holes (Figure 14) allow the birds in and out. Interestingly, in the gable end of the adjoining house, another small series of holes can be seen high in the gable (Figure 15) and probably lead into a small pigeon loft in the roof space and undoubtedly reached via a trap-door in the ceiling, a not uncommon arrangement found in other late-eighteenth century or nineteenth century examples, especially in the West Riding of Yorkshire.

At *Foulsyke Farm,* Scalby (Figure 16), a dovecote is contained in the tower which rises above the large impressive entrance gate at the side. Erected in red brick with an ornate eaves course supporting a tiled roof, it has four pigeon holes in the upper storey above a glazed round-headed window at second floor level with a small glazed door on the ground floor.

A second dovecote of this period can also be found at Scalby. In 1885, the eccentric Edwin Brough had built in red brick Scalby

Figure 14. Court Green, Cloughton. Detail of the pigeon holes in the apex of an outbuilding dated 1859.

Photograph Alan Whitworth, courtesy Yorkshire Dovecote Society

Figure 15. Court Green, Cloughton. Pigeon holes high in a gable end lead into a pigeon loft.

Photograph Alan Whitworth, courtesy Yorkshire Dovecote Society

Manor in the nineteenth century 'Queen Anne' style for his new bride. He also saw to it that extensive kennels were erected for his pack of bloodhounds, two of which, Burgho and Barnaby became famous for being used to track the notorious nineteenth century 'Jack the Ripper' during the period of the Whitechapel murders in London. Incorporated into these kennels at the rear of Scalby Manor, is a dovecote of modest proportions which sadly lack their next boxes.

Finally, I should like to conclude by mentioning a small number of dovecotes which have now disappeared and include one at Gristhorpe mentioned in 1601. This stood in 'Dovecote Close' opposite the manor house. The pigeon house here still existed in 1744 when it was referred to in a dispute over a footpath right of way across Dovecote Close. It was demolished sometime in the late-eighteenth or early-nineteenth century.

Figure 16. Foulsyke Farm, Scalby. A nineteenth century entrance gate with dovecote in the adjoining tower. *Photograph Alan Whitworth, courtesy Yorkshire Dovecote Society*

Two other examples worth mentioning are the excavated dovecotes at Ayton Castle, near Scarborough, whose ruins owned by English Heritage, are open to the public, and Allerston Hall/Manor.

At Ayton, excavations were carried out by the Scarborough and District Archaeological Society, and a free-standing circular dovecote was discovered some two hundred feet to the east of the present tower. Digging revealed nearly five feet of the building remained. The surviving wall was three metres wide at ground level increasing by three inches immediately above the footings. The curvature of the wall indicated a diameter of twenty-five feet. The stones of the dovecote were squared on the outer surface, set in clay and both sides face-pointed with plaster, some of which still existed. A small, two feet wide doorway was located to the south-east.

On the inside of the walling three rows of nesting holes remained; the base of the lowest being twenty-one inches above floor level which was flagged for a distance of twelve inches from the wall. The base of the next row of holes was ten inches higher and the top remaining row fourteen inches higher still. Beneath each nest hole was a protruding ledge upon which the birds could alight. The nest holes averaged eighteen inches in depth from the edge of the alighting ledge made of slabbed stone which stood out about three inches from the wall.

The entrance to the nest holes was between seven and eight inches wide by five and nine inches high. The lowest row turned to the left in an L-shape, the next row to the right, the third row to the left again and no doubt this alternation was the pattern throughout - a common feature in many medieval dovecotes. The nesting holes were notably different in size and those exposed averaged about two feet apart horizontally. It was calculated that with an internal diameter of eighteen feet six inches and a height of twenty feet, the Ayton dovecote would probably have held about six hundred nest boxes.

There was no sign of a potence or internal revolving ladder by which means access could be gained to the nest boxes to collect eggs and young squabs, instead, at the centre of the floor was a circular stone structure measuring four feet two inches wide internally, which was sunk fifteen inches into the ground. It had a compacted red earth base, and as it contained no guano it is thought that it must have had some form of cover, and speculation is that it was a food trough as it is doubtful whether it would have retained water. Stretching from this trough to the inside of the dovecote wall was a layer of bird droppings a foot deep still with the active smell of the poultry-house; this layer also contained a considerable number of pigeon bones.

Inside the pigeon house and also immediately on the outside was a mass of building stone together with a great quantity of large limestone slabs, thought to be alighting ledges, and stone roofing tiles. Obviously the roof had been so tiled, and on the collapse of the building no attempt had been made at rebuilding. No pottery shards of a later date than mid-fourteenth century were found associated with the dovecote, and it seems to have become disused halfway through this century and there are surface indications that another larger pigeon house was erected further up the hill.[12]

Finally, at Allerston Hall, two pigeon houses existed, the first to the north of the hall, near to the old estate boundary, where a circular, free-standing dovecote

Figure 17. Sleights (near Whitby). An interesting series of pigeon holes leading into a gable pigeon loft. *Photograph Alan Whitworth, courtesy Yorkshire Dovecote Society*

was uncovered during archaeological work on the hall site. It measured internally eighteen feet, and the remaining walls varied in width from four feet to five feet, unfortunately they were not high enough to show evidence of the nesting arrangements.[13]

The second, and larger dovecote was located to the south of Allerston Hall. Here, the external diameter was twenty-five feet at soil level and twenty-six feet at the base, with walls measuring four feet thick. The nest holes had been built, surprisingly, right down to the floor, a disadvantage and likely to become blocked up by bird droppings, but the mistake had been rectified by stopping up the lower holes and the first row of open nest holes stood two feet six inches from the floor.

There were four rows of nest holes still surviving, and all but the lowest one had a protruding alighting ledge immediately beneath. The holes averaged in measurement six inches by four inches across their entrance and were approximately twenty inches deep, L-shaped as is common, but with all the rows turning to the left rather than alternating which is the usual arrangement. There appears to have been some sixteen holes in each row, calculated on a dovecote of twenty foot in height, to total about three hundred nest boxes. There was a narrow doorway to the north-west. The date of the dovecote was thought to be thirteenth century.[14]

Archaeological excavation, field-work and research of documents are three methods of locating dovecotes, and it is probable that a systematic search of historical records would provide evidence to the existence of many more examples of pigeon houses which can be then added to the growing total of known dovecotes and pigeon lofts of the East Coast.

Notes and References

1. Farmer, P.G. 'A Dovecote at Brompton', *Dalesman*, Vol.42, March 1981.
2. *ibid.*
3. *ibid.*
4. NYCRO, Reg. Deeds AK, 1760-64; BKS, 1781-83.
5. NYCRO, Reg. Deeds BF, 1774-76; BM, 1777-78.
6. NYCRO, Reg. Deeds ZQV 2/2.
7. Young, Reverend George *History of Whitby*, Vol.I, 1817.
8. NYCRO, Reg. Deeds ZF 4/3/1.
9. Ryedale Historian, No.16, 1992-93.
10. Young *History of Whitby*, Vol.I, 1817.
11. *ibid*, Vol.II, 1817.
12. Rimmington, F C & Rutter, J G Scarborough & District Archaeological Society Research Report No.5, 1967.
13. Transactions of the Scarborough & District Archaeological Society, Vol.2, No.9, 1966.
14. *ibid.* Vol.2, No.12, 1969.

10. ANNIE'S TALE – MEMORIES OF LIFE IN WHITBY

by Annie Parker

MOTHER USED TO BOIL CRABS for my Granny Wood (Figure 1) to sell. She scrubbed the crabs and boiled them in a big boiler, and in order to heat the water she had to make a fire underneath by shovelling wood and coal into the grate and lighting it with burning paper or straw. The boiler stood in a wooden shed near Grandad Wood's Kipper House at the top of Henrietta Street and my cousins and I would sit up on the grass under the East Cliff, just above the hut, waiting for the little crab's claws that were left after the last boiling.

Mother (Figure 2) also did her washing here once a week, after she cleaned the boiler out and

Figure 1. Martha Hannah Wood, 'Granny Wood'.

Figure 2. Annie Parker's mother as a young girl

made it spotless. She had to walk to the top of the street where the water tap was in order to fill buckets, which she then had to carry back to the boiler for both the washing and the rinsing. She did the rinsing in a 'poss' tub. Of course she had to go through the same procedure of carrying heavy buckets of water when she was boiling crabs.

When mother washed sheets, she would lie them out on the sands to dry (Figure 3). She would put a stone on each corner to hold them down and then would leave my sister to sit with them. The sand in those days was soft and silvery and lovely and clean and dry.

The family of Fortune's who had the kipper house further along the street (Figure 4) also owned donkeys, and after being on the sands, the donkeys were brought up the street and when the mothers heard the bells which they wore on their heads, they would bring out their little ones to give them a ride.

A young man living in Whitby used to play with 'Tangle Sticks'[1] on an empty oil drum. He was so expert at it that a visitor to the town once offered him a job in a band.

When we first came to live in Henrietta Street (Figure 5) we only had a little room to live in which had a 'bed spot' as it was called, which was a small alcove in the wall where the bed would fit. There was no indoor water, and we had to get water from a tap outside, which was on the other side of the street, and we did not have our own toilet. The lady from whom we rented our single

Figure 3. Tate Hill Sands, beneath St Mary's church. It was here that in the 19th century a Russian ship ran aground, which incident became a central feature in Bram Stoker's epic novel, *Dracula*. It was here, also, that women dried their washing on the sands.

Figure 4. Fortune's Kipper Smoke House and shop, Henrietta Street. Today, one of the last remaining 'Smoke Houses' in the street and famous the world over.

Figure 5. Henrietta Street today; only the lower end remains, where the cottages and roadway have been much improved.

room lived in a house which was situated down our passage and we had to go through her house to get to the toilet which was in the backyard. Later, mother bought the house so that my sister and I had a bedroom. Before this my sister had to sleep out with various grannies and aunts.

Mother had to *scane* (open) mussels early in the morning. To do this she would sit on a chair with the mussels on a long, deep heavy metal tray in front of her with one end resting on her lap and the other end perched on a second chair. There was a pot of some sort on the tray to drop

Figure 5. Whitby harbour in the 1950s showing fishermen mending nets in the traditional manner.

the mussels in, and by her side was a bath to hold the mussels shells. The shelled mussels, which were bait for the fishing lines, were then put into a bucket and placed under a running tap till they were swollen and ready to be put on the hooks of the fishing lines. These lines she coiled round and round, with the bait to the front on a *cain* (skep) till the pile was quite high.

Then dad would tie the whole thing together and put it on a handcart ready to be trundled down the steep bank and over the bridge to the coble the next day. The baited lines were so heavy that mother could only carried the empty ones from the days fishing. Every line was furnished with well over one hundred hooks set at six feet distance from each other and a number of lines were fastened together and used at once. These extended to about three miles when set out at sea. When the boat returned mother would carry one used line on each arm back up the steep bank home before she set to and cooked the dinner (Figure 6).

Figure 6. Annie Parker as a young woman carrying fishing lines on her head.

After dinner mother and dad would clean off all the pieces of bait and seaweed left on the hooks in order to get it ready to bait the next day. I was always scared of getting caught by a hook, as dad used to fling the empty hooks about so very quickly when coiling them onto the skep. This kind of accident, which was quite a common occurrence, was taken care of by an uncle who lived with us, who was an expert in removing them from anyone's arms or legs if it so happened. He would use a cork, working at it to get the hook out somehow, as he always said they made a mess of it at the hospital.

I hated the smell of mussels, and if mum and dad were doing the lines when I came home from school at dinnertime, I'd knock on the window to let them know and then go back to school without my dinner. I liked it best when dad went salmon fishing.

Figure 7. 'The Landslip at Whitby' showing Henrietta Street after a large part of the cliff and churchyard above crashed down onto the houses below in the winter of 1871. *The Graphic*, 21 January 1871

As dad and uncle Albert had to be up at four o'clock in the morning to go to sea, my sister and I had to be home before nine o'clock at night as, after the nine o'clock news on the wireless had finished, we had to go to bed. Dad's fishermen friends used to come round and play cards around seven o'clock in the evening, and I don't think they played for money either. Refreshments were pint pots of water!

Granny and Granddad Wood, mother's parents, lived in a house which was the only remaining one, right at the top of Henrietta Street. Because of subsidence it was leaning badly, just like the leaning tower of Pisa. Granny and granddad eventually had to move, and the top floor of the house was then taken off as it was considered dangerous. As children, we played in the bottom part which was left standing, and I remember the fireplace was still there in its old place (Figures 7 & 8).

After Christmas we would take up our old holly tree, still with bits of tinsel on it, and put it in the old building. My cousin had a goat and he used to tether it on the green nearby which we called the 'Old Battery', and the goat would break free and get into the old house and eat all the leaves which were left on the holly tree. The following day there would be nothing left, not even the tinsel.

When we were playing in the old house we would barricade ourselves inside, piling up old herring boxes against the huge heavy door to keep the goat out. One day it got loose and crossed the bridge and a policeman brought it back on a great long rope. We were scared of the goat but a young man who, unfortunately, still had the mentality of a child, used to stand with it and knock his pipe out on its horns. He did have tobacco in the pipe but it was never lit.

Granny and Granddad Wood had a fish business curing herrings, and mother's four sisters all worked in granny's herring houses splitting open the herrings and spiking them on long poles after they had been soaked in brine. They then hung the fish up ready for smoking. Granddad would go to the saw-mill for wood shavings and sawdust for the fires. He used to take my sister and I on his open cart to Sandsend. The little pony who pulled the cart was named Polly, and when granddad had had a drink or two, and Polly was roaming loose on the grass on the 'Battery', she wouldn't come to him when he called her. She would wait until he was near and then slide down the sloping cliff on her backside away from him. He would have to get mother to catch her.

Granddad had once taken a few drinks and was coming down the street with his cart, when mother came out of the house and noticed there was something wrong with Polly. She realised that the pony's halter was on back to front - the pony looked like pictures of Queen Elizabeth I with a high ruff behind its neck. Mum halted granddad, who said, 'It's a good job you stopped me, lass, or I would have got locked up!'

On election day, granddad would go out to work with his cart decorated in his own political parties colours, but when he came in for dinner, granny would go out and pull the lot off and do it up again in the colours of her own party as she was of a different political persuasion.

Figure 8. Among the buildings destroyed was Mr Harland's pipe factory and the Wesleyan Methodist Church. The landslip was virtually a repeat of the events of a century previous. The *Graphic*, 21 January 1871

Mother was married at sixteen and she had an awfully hard life being the wife of a fisherman. Dad only got a lad's wage and he was paid the same even if he was called out in the lifeboat. When I was a baby, mother used to walk to Robin Hood's Bay to gather *cuvins* (winkles) to get the money to buy my sister shoes. Mother was quite small and only weighed seven stones, yet she had to go down onto the Scar gather the winkles, and then had to carry them in a sack on her back up the bank to the railway station where they would get weighed and be left to be transported by rail to their destination.

After being paid she had to walk back home again. An oldish man once said to her, 'Put thi' best foot forrard, lass, and we'll see how long it takes us.' The church clock was just striking the hour when they got back to Whitby, which showed that it had just taken them one hour to walk the five or six miles from Robin Hood's Bay.

When we were little we loved to sleep in Granny Wood's front bedroom where my cousins and I used to all pile into the one big bed. There seemed to be lots of mattresses on it. Granny used to go gathering *cuvins* before granddad got the little fish shop on Sandgate. She came home one day and mother (then a tiny child) was poorly, and my granny sat with her for hours in her wet clothes until she developed pneumonia.

Mother told us of the wreck of the hospital ship the *Rohilla* under the East Cliff in 1914 (Figure 9 and 10). She said it was a terrible stormy night, but her brothers went out onto the Scar to try and rescue some of the people who were washing about in the sea.

One of her brothers had hold of one person in his arms when a huge sea broke over them both and took the man away out of his hands. Mother said her brother was heartbroken.

She said it was awful hearing the siren on the *Rohilla* sounding mournfully all night long. The Whitby people couldn't believe their eyes next morning when they looked out and the harbour was full of

Figure 9. The hospital ship *Rhohilla*, which was sunk off Whitby with the loss of many lives.

white wood right up to the top of the piers. Everything in the ship would be brand new as it was a newly launched ship on its maiden voyage. Many of the people who were drowned were doctors and nurses.

The ship should never have been so far inshore and so near to the rocks. Mother was told that the captain walked safely off the Scar wrapped in a big cloak.

Mother's uncle, who was a fisherman, was a member of the lifeboat crew which once had to pull the lifeboat [*Robert Whitworth*] round the cliff tops from Whitby to Robin Hood's Bay in order to rescue a stranded crew from a shipwreck. The storm was so terrible and the sea too rough to allow the men to row the boat out of Whitby harbour. One of our great-great-grandfathers got a Certificate of Honour which mother had hanging in a frame on her sitting-room wall. He had gone down the East Cliff on a rope with a light to shine on the scene so that the crew of a shipwrecked schooner could be rescued.

Dad's father was drowned in the sea just off Whitby. The fishermen fished from small cobbles with a single sail, and his boat was caught in a sudden squall. Mother said that granddad had told her that the mast he usually used was broken, and that the one he had as a spare didn't fit properly. She thinks the sail had gone too far over the side causing the boat to capsize. Granddad's body was never recovered, and dad never got over it. Mother said he cried every time he passed the area of sea where his father's boat turned over.

During the last war a mine got caught in dad's fishing net and it exploded. He didn't go fishing anymore after that.

A bomb was also dropped on Whitby from a German airplane and landed on the place where the Gas Board had their offices in Flowergate near to Woolworth's. The area is now occupied by a supermarket. I was working at Woolworth's then, and I remember we hid under the counters and could hear the sound of breaking glass all around us. My mother had run out of the house when she heard the bang, and was told that the bomb had dropped on Woolworth's. 'Oh!' she cried, 'Our Anne works there!' and she ran into town to find me. She was so overjoyed that I was safe.

Dad's family lived on the Crag, up Arguments Yard, in a tenement building. Dad used to take my sister and I to visit granny on Sunday mornings. She had the top flat and a view all over the East Side. Six to eight families lived at the top end of Arguments Yard.

When my family lived on Henrietta Street the family living opposite were very violent and I was always terrified of them. The father, when drunk, would throw his sons down the stairs onto the street, and the sons used to fight in the road just outside our window. Eventually the family moved away to live down the Ghaut.[2] The woman of the family would stand outside the entrance to the Ghaut and howl like a dog when she was drunk.

Another family lived in a block further up our street along a dark passage and they had to climb up an unlit staircase to their home. If it was dark, the husband used to shout his wife's name, and she showed a light or came down the steps to meet him when he called. One old woman who lived on the street used to go onto the beach or the Scar to collect lumps of chalk which she would sell to folks to rub on their front doorsteps and stone window ledges. It was the fashion then to scour the front doorstep with white chalk to make it look good.

At Christmas several of the older women in the street would go into the countryside visiting out of the way places. They would carry a little box with a tiny doll in it. This was supposed to be the 'Christ-child', and the women would sing the 'Vessel Cup Song' (a Christmas greeting), after which they would receive some money, for this custom was said to bring good luck.

I remember one of them coming to our house to sing when she was drunk, but mother was out, and so my sister told her to go away. The old woman was most annoyed and said, 'Your mother wouldn't have done that.'

When we lived in the house in Henrietta Street my mother kept hens out at the back under the East Cliff. There she also kept the old wartime Anderson shelter for their run and to keep the rain off. In summer the hens would roam about along the grassy bank under the cliff where they would lay their eggs. Mother would sometimes find quite a lot, but she wouldn't use them all, as she didn't know how old some of them were. However, an older man living nearby was glad of them.

Figure 10. The wreck of the hospital ship *Rohilla* and the lifeboat (left) which was also destroyed.

I remember in winter she made a hot mash for the hens, putting in some karswood, a powder which was supposed to keep the birds laying all the time. I don't think it did! She would bring newly hatched downy chicks into the house to keep warm by the coal fire. I remember in summer when the fire was not in use one of the hens would come indoors and settle in the empty fire grate to lay an egg.

By this time we had a tap in the backyard, which was one step up from the door. One day after continuous rain mother opened the door and water gushed into the house because the outside sink had blocked up and overflowed. The boot polish box was floating about in the water!

At dinnertime on a Saturday mother would send us down the road to a little shop to buy homemade meat pies, then we would call at another shop a few doors away for a jug of homemade soup. I wasn't keen on either of these - I liked mother's best. The people who made the pies had another shop opposite where they sold fancy cakes, as we called them.

At another shop we could buy sweets, and the lady who sold them made a dark-coloured mint which locals called 'Betsy's Mint Kisses'. There was a grocers shop called Ditchburn's, where Shepherds Purse is now, and they sold lardy flat cakes which we called 'Ditchburn's Bread Buns'.

When my mother's fisherfolk relatives came to see us from Hartlepool they always took some back home with them, along with Johnson's saveloys. At the corner of Church Street Wilcox's had a store, and I remember the little cups in which the shop assistants put your money in before they clipped them onto wires set high up over people's heads. These wires carried the cups across the shop to a small boxed affair at one end where the cashier sat. She would then send your change back across the shop in the little cup.

There was a chemist shop at the top of Bridge Street and at the other end was Tyler's shoe shop where we bought sand slippers (plimsolls) for one shilling and eleven pence. Unfortunately, one day the shop set on fire and Tyler's had to move into Baxtergate. The Co-operative grocery store was on Sandgate and if you wrote out your order and gave it to the assistant, your groceries would be delivered by van on the Saturday. There were three butcher's shops on Sandgate and a pub, and there was a fruit shop on the corner.

Mum and dad liked to go to the pictures on Saturday night, and Woolworth's, where I worked, used to keep open in the evening as lots of people would call in for a quarter of sweets when on their way to the 'first house'. There were two showings of the film every night, 'first and second house'. On Saturday nights the cinemas were always packed to capacity. There were three picture houses in Whitby, the Empire, the Colliseum, and the Waterloo. Before she went to the picture house mother would make up a huge bowl of ginger beer for us - it always smelt lovely.

When we were of school age quite a few families would walk on to Saltwick Bay for a picnic on Sundays in summer and it is only a few years back since my cousin and her family stopped going. That was when the holiday chalets were built and Saltwick became a summer holiday camp.

Before we got to Saltwick there was a gap in the cliff which we called the 'Gardens' and there was a little hut down below which a lady opened up in summer to sell teas. I remember a goat was tied up there; I expect it was for milk.

There were lots of characters in Whitby in the old days. A little hunch-backed woman lived in the street and the fishermen thought she brought bad luck. If they met her as they were going off to sea they would turn back and set out later.

A lovely woman lived near us, and when I had what they called 'Double Pneumonia' when I was small, she would bring me little things to play with. Another lovely lady who we called 'Aunty' used to sell trinkets which she brought, I think, from the country I still recall an oldish man coming round with a basket on his head from which he sold damaged fruit. Mother would buy William Pears from him.

The milkman would bring milk twice a day from his farm. He had a churn to carry it in with a measuring jug hanging inside. The milk was always lovely and fresh, straight from the cow. A farmer's wife whose name was Mary, used to come down from the country with fresh butter to sell and she would bring some to our house.

Saturday was Market Day when the farm folk brought produce to sell in Whitby Market Place. The farmers killed their cows in a place round the back of the Market Square which was originally under a tenement building, but they moved later to another spot nearby. They would herd the cattle down Church Lane and if we children were in the street at the time, we would run up the nearest yard to keep out of there way.

Another character living in Whitby was a priest called Aaron Williams who seemed to know all the legal ins and outs; and if anyone was putting up a wall which he knew was against conservation laws, he would pull it down as the people were building it. Mother said all the children would follow him as soon as he was 'on the march'.

The fisherfolk all seemed to have nicknames. Dad's was 'Hardy', but I don't know why as he wasn't a tough person. Another fisherman was called 'Wood Peg' for some reason and an old woman in the street was nicknamed 'Hannah Tricky'; she used to say that empty tins kept the fire bright.

Hannah Tricky had a son called 'Go Go' and together they would go down and buy fish from the fish quay and load it on to a small cart to sell. Granddad Wood used to do the same and take it to his shop on Sandgate where Auntie Peg helped him. It was her sons who eventually took over the fish business after she died. When mother and her three sisters were alive I used to watch them picking crabs round a table in the same room where they are still sold today.

In summer an old blind beggar man sat on a stool at the bottom of Khyber Pass Steps. He was usually knitting as he begged though how he managed to knit I do not know. Dad was very friendly with him and would give him fish. One day dad said to Blind Billy, 'I took you some fish round last night, but you hadn't the light on, so I thought you weren't in.' Billy replied, 'What would I want with a light on?' Dad was a long time living that one down.

At Easter, whole families used to walk to Glen Esk so that the children could roll their Easter Eggs down the hill. We didn't have chocolate ones then, just hard boiled hen's eggs which we dyed different colours - yellow, green, blue and red. A lady in Henrietta Street used to sell them ready coloured and she also sold such things as sweets which she put in the window of her living room.

In summer she and her husband would take a churn of ice-cream on to Saltwick Bay on a barrow, or sometimes a cart, and there they would sell cornets and ice-cream sandwiches. There would be enough people out there at Saltwick on Sundays in the summer months to make it worthwhile, but it must have been hard work to get the heavy churn along Church Lane, walking all the way, and then having to get it down the uneven cliff walk at Saltwick. Of course it would be worse still having to haul it back up at the end of the day.

Notes and References

1. Tangle-sticks; the strong stems of the kelp seaweed, which are left on the beach after the tide.
2. Ghaut or Ghaunt. A local name for a narrow passage or steps leading down to a river; a landing place. It is pronounced 'Gort'.

11. THE STORY OF THE WHITBY LIFEBOAT ROBERT WHITWORTH

by Alan Whitworth

FORTY-SIX YEARS AFTER THE FORMATION of the Royal National Lifeboat Institute (RNLI) by Sir William Hillary on 4 March 1824, the lifeboat *Robert Whitworth* commenced service in Whitby, a small fishing port on the east coast of North Yorkshire surrounded by some of the most treacherous and dangerous waters around the British Isles.

In the seventy years between the first lifeboat setting out at Whitby and the lifeboat *Robert Whitworth* arriving in January 1870, it is known that at least 129 lives were saved off the coast hereabouts by the previous five lifeboats. In the ten years that the Robert Whitworth served the lifeboat and crew saved no less than 126 people, and in the history of the lifeboat at Whitby, the service of the *Robert Whitworth* was possibly the most significant and glamorous of all the boats ever on station. No other rowing lifeboat ever saved as many lives; and it was during the existence of the *Robert Whitworth* at Whitby, that probably the bravest and most spectacular rescue ever undertaken by a lifeboat of the RNLI took place.

The origins of the name *Robert Whitworth* lay in Manchester, where indeed, during the early years of the RNLI, much sterling work was done by this city to promote and foster an interest in this noble institution. It was there that the first 'Lifeboat Saturday' was held, when in October 1891, Saturday crowds in Manchester and Salford were startled to see two lifeboats and their crews, mounted on carts, being dragged through the streets before proceeding to the Pleasure Gardens at Belle Vue where the lifeboats were launched on the lake before an audience of 300,000 spectators, many of whom

Figure 1. Nineteenth century sketch drawing of Pier Road prior to 1895 showing the harbour master's office/house (centre) and the two RNLI lifeboat houses (left and right, with large black doors).

had never set eyes on the sea! That first 'Lifeboat Saturday', now held annually, raised £5,500.

Yet even before that day, the work of the Manchester Branch of the RNLI had not gone unnoticed, and it was because of the outstanding contribution of this regional branch, with Treasurer, Robert Whitworth, who by 1892 had attained the position of Vice-President, that the RNLI named the Whitby boat in his honour. Indeed, by 1864, no less than four lifeboats had been funded by the Manchester Committee under the auspices of *Robert Whitworth,* and at least two boats sailed under his name - the one at Whitby and

Figure 2. A detail from the 1893 Ordnance Survey Map of Scotch Head and Pier Road showing the location of the two lifeboat houses in greater detail. The one adjoining Pier House was a wooden shed which housed No.2 Lifeboat and was replaced in 1895 with the present Lifeboat House (now Museum). The other lifeboat house (bottom) was for the No.1 Lifeboat.

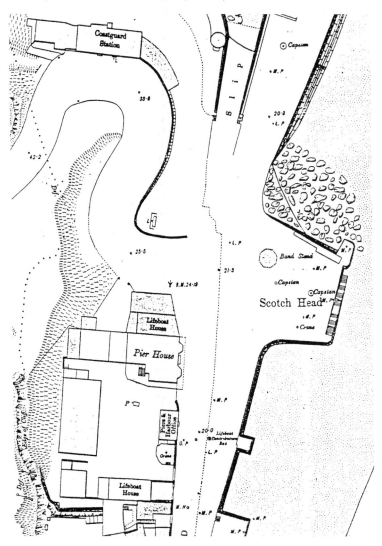

initially, another at Bridlington which was delivered there in November 1864.

Unfortunately, however, at Bridlington, the lifeboat *Robert Whitworth* of 1864 fared badly, proving difficult to launch and handle in the sea conditions prevalent to that town. The boat, disliked by the Bridlington lifeboatmen was ultimately sent away to Whitehaven in 1866. A replacement lifeboat of the same name in 1871, proved equally unsuitable in the Bridlington waters, and, likewise, was soon taken off station and replaced by a craft which was specially designed to meet the particular needs of that Yorkshire port.

The removal of the *Robert Whitworth* from Bridlington presented the RNLI in London with a problem. In Manchester, Robert Whitworth and his friends had been extremely active on the Institute's behalf, and by 1871 had succeeded in raising funds for over fifteen lifeboats and arranging their displacement around the coast of Britain. In order that Robert Whitworth and his work should continue to be perpetuated as quickly as possible and so as not to cause offence, it was decided that an existing lifeboat should be renamed to ensure the proper recognition of their efforts.

In Whitby, following a particularly hazardous rescue in 1869 by the local lifeboat, *Lucy*, so much damage was sustained that it was thought prudent to replace her, and in January 1870, the *Lucy* was replaced by a brand-new, ten-oared, self-righting lifeboat which cost £248 7s 6d with her launching carriage costing an additional £100 10s 0d.

Initially, the new lifeboat on arrival at Whitby was unnamed and was known locally as a consequence, by the unofficial title of her predecessor. However, at a meeting of the RNLI's Committee of Management on 22 February 1871, it was decided to officially transfer the name *Robert Whitworth* to the Whitby lifeboat following their predicament at Bridlington and so end the Institute's dilemma.

The National Lifeboat Institute, knowing the dangerous nature of the coastal waters hereabouts, at this time, wisely provided Whitby with three lifeboats - two stationed in the town, and one about a mile along the coast to the north between Whitby and Sandsend at Upgang and known by the name of Upgang lifeboat. The three RNLI lifeboats at that period were fitted with the most modern and improved equipment for saving life; and Whitby could boast of one of the best lifeboat-houses in England. In addition, for inshore rescue, a contingent of the Coastguard Service was stationed at Whitby with rockets, lines and breeches buoys to enable rescues to take place from the pier and cliff-tops - and there was also a fourth lifeboat, privately owned by the fishermen themselves.

While all three services were independent of each other, the RNLI, the Coastguard and the fishermen, in practice often co-ordinated rescue attempts under the direction of the Lifeboat Secretary, however, there were times when they operated in conflict which could cause no little sense of ill-feeling in such a tight-knit community. The RNLI lifeboats were numbered one and two, and took turns to go out, although lifeboat No.1 was considered the lead craft and took precedence at launches, an important consideration for the crews who received a renumeration for attending rescues.

It was because of the number of lifeboats stationed at Whitby and the type of incident which dictated the method of rescue attempt, that it was not until 26 July 1870, that the *Robert Whitworth* undertook her first rescue, six months into her service, when she helped to save the brigantine *Mary & Jane*, of Sunderland, and the crew of four; and it was not until late the following year, that the *Robert Whitworth* was involved in another rescue when on 2 October 1871, she was launched to assist the schooner *Dispatch*, of Whitby, which was seen in a distressed condition off the harbour. In this instance, the schooner was 'drove over the rocks into the broken water. The master immediately showed a signal of distress, [and] the

Figure 3. A nineteenth century illustration of the lifeboat *Robert Whitworth* in action off the coast of Whitby.

No.1 life-boat, *Robert Whitworth* was quickly launched, and proceeded to the schooner; and after the life-boat men had succeeded in getting her anchor and towing her into a safe position, the master and crew of two men left her, she being in a leak state at the time, and they were safely landed in the life-boat through a heavy sea.'

> *The next morning the vessel was still [seen] riding at her anchor, and as there seemed some hope of saving her, the wind being fair, although the sea was very heavy, the life-boat* Robert Whitworth *placed the master and crew on board, and, with assistance, the schooner was taken on to Hartlepool.*[1]

The *Robert Whitworth* next saw action on 6 December 1871, when 'several fishing-cobbles off Whitby were making for the land, during a severe north-east wind and a heavy sea . . . being dangerous for the boats to enter the harbour, the No.2 old life-boat [*Petrel*] was launched. She succeeded in rescuing the crew of two of the cobbles, numbering six men, and landed them safely on the beach. That life-boat, however, could not go off again, as during her cruise she had sprung a leak, and a good deal of water had got into her. The No.1 life-boat *Robert Whitworth*, was then launched, and proceeded to the rescue of the four other cobbles, which had, in the meantime, reached the 'Roads'. The crews of these boats, numbering twelve, were rescued and landed in safety. he prompt manner in which the life-boats were manned and launched was very creditable to all parties concerned.'[2] 'Six cobbles were afterwards washed on to the beach in a very damaged state, most of their gear and all their fish being lost'.[3]

Following the multiple rescue in December 1871, incredibly it was another four years before the *Robert Whitworth* put out to save any further souls, which occurred on the Monday afternoon of 18 October 1875, when the 'barque *Teazer*, of Whitby, 293 tons register, owned by Mr John Harrison Storm, Esk Terrace, and commanded by his son, Mr William Storm, came on shore near the West Pier. She was from London in ballast for Whitby for dock. The master states he arrived off this port about 2pm, the wind blowing a fresh gale from the SSE. About 4pm he saw the sea breaking over the pier ends, and thinking there was too much sea for him to enter the harbour in safety, he put the vessel's head to sea with the intention of standing off until the weather moderated. However, the steam-tug *Emu* went out to his assistance and took the vessel in tow. In response to a signal from the master of the tug for sail to be taken off the ship, the sails were furled. The ship then drifted to leeward and the master finding the tug had not power to tow her within the piers, and she touching the ground outside the West Pier, he let go the towline, and hoisted fore-stay-sail, [and] braced the yards to endeavour to cant the vessel's head to sea, but before anything could be done the vessel drifted with the heavy sea behind the West Pier, on to the sands, where she still lies. The Royal Institution's lifeboat, *Robert Whitworth*, was promptly launched for the rescue of nine hands, and they were soon safely landed on the beach near the slipway. A rocket had previously been fired by the Coastguard from the Pier, but it fell just outside the ship. During the week when weather and tide permitted men have been employed in striping and unrigging the stranded vessel. It is expected she will be got off next spring tides if the weather moderates'.[4]

A few days later, the *Robert Whitworth*, undertook another rescue, when 'on Wednesday [20 October] about noon, when a gale of wind was blowing and a tremendous sea [was] running a dismasted barque was descried some miles to the south of this port, apparently helplessly drifting to the north, but at too great a distance for the best telescopes to make out whether there was any one on board or whether she had been altogether abandoned. There was soon a large number of people congregated on the piers, and the greatest excitement prevailed. It being low water, Captain Forrest of the steam-tug, *Emu*, could not get out of the harbour, or he would have tried to fetch in the disabled vessel. The brave fishermen who man our life-boats were in readiness to launch their No.1 boat, the *Robert Whitworth*, belonging to the Royal National Institution, should there be any signs of life discovered on board the barque. This, however, could not be decided from the shore, so they determined to go and see.'

Shortly before two o'clock the boat was launched with her hardy crew, who gallantly pulled through or over surging breakers . . . The men are well immured by the arduous and precarious occupation of fishermen to battling with the sea, and having the greatest confidence in their boat and her commander (Mr S Lacy, coxswain) they know no fear when on an errand of mercy, while the hope of saving life nerves their arms to do feats of strength which in ordinary work would be utterly impossible.

After a laborious and perilous voyage of some miles they came up with the disabled vessel, which proved to be the barque Godstadt Minde, *of Tonsberg, laden with deals and her deck cargo still remaining. The lifeboat pulled alongside and finding that she had been abandoned left her to her fate, and pulled for the shore. Both the barque and the life-boat were lost to sight from this port during the afternoon, and as darkness came on there was the intentest concern manifested in all quarters for the safety of the crew of the boat, as the rain began to fall in torrents and the weather in other respects showed no signs of moderating. The fears were allayed, however, a little before six o'clock, by the receipt of a telegram at the Coastguard Station, announcing the welcome news that the lifeboat's crew had safely effected a landing at Runswick, a little before darkness came on. From the inhabitants of Runswick generally they received every kindness, and to Dr Laverick, of Hinderwell, who happened to be at the place, the men express their deepest gratitude for his assiduous and thoughtful attention to their wants.*

After a much needed rest and refreshment, the [life]*boat was placed in a safe position, and conveyances were procured in which the crew were brought to their homes at Whitby. During the night the barque* [Godstadt Minde] *drove on shore between Staithes and Skinningrove.*[5]

Following this rescue, there was an interesting postscript to the episode the conclusion of which, resulted in not a little controversy in the town and cause some amount of ill-feeling between the fishermen toward the lifeboat crew for a considerable time afterwards.

The attack was first launched in an open letter to the 'Secretary of the National Lifeboat Institution, London' printed in the *Whitby Gazette,* and concerned an incident which took place two days later when the crew of the *Robert Whitworth* where engaged in another rescue, the substance of which was recounted in the local newspaper.

The barque [Godstadt Minde], *as reported in our last, went ashore north of Staithes during Wednesday night, after having been found to have been abandoned by the Whitby lifeboat, which bravely put off to assist her crew had they been still on board. Night coming on, the lifeboat crew put into Runswick, where they left the boat, and came to Whitby by road . . . On Friday, the crew walked over to Runswick to bring back the lifeboat, and when nearing Whitby* [by sea] *a barque was observed flying a flag for assistance, and they proceeded to her. John Douglas, pilot, also put off with his new mule, well-manned to render assistance. The vessel proved to be a Norwegian barque with her ballast canted, and the lifeboat crew bravely undertook to proceed to the north, and endeavour to get her into port, and nobly succeeded in reaching East Hartlepool in safety at half-past nine o'clock the* same night. *Douglas returned to Whitby and succeeded in reaching the harbour in safety, although at great risk. The latter lifeboat service has given offence to some of the fishermen of this port* [Whitby], *who consider that the Institution's boat had no right to be used in the salvage of property, and that it was contrary to the rules of the Institution for the coxswain (Mr S Lacy) to allow the boat to be used so. They have drawn the attention of the Lifeboat Institution to the matter, and it has been investigated by the local Committee.*[6]

THE WHITBY COBBLEMEN AND THE NATIONAL LIFE-BOATS

We have been requested to publish the following letter, which has been transmitted to its destination this week.

Whitby, 25th October 1875

Sir,- *On the 22nd Inst, the barque* Svadsfare, *of Porsgrund, came off Whitby, making signals of distress, about 3pm. A pilot cobble with five men and a branch pilot in company put off in heavy sea at the risk of their lives to render assistance, and succeeded in reaching the vessel. At the same time the National Life-boat No.1,* Robert Whitworth, *came alongside, and took possession of the ship. The coxswain left his boat and acted as branch pilot, and turned the cobble and her crew adrift, not caring whether they reached the harbour or not. As soon as the coxswain of the life-boat was on board, the ship's head was turned to shore, with the apparent intention of running her on to the beach. The cobble again came alongside, and asked what they were going to do with the ship, and were told that they were going to run her ashore. They (the cobblemen) replied, "Don't do that, as we are willing to come on board and help you get her to a northern port"; whereupon, they* [the lifeboatmen] *put her about, and proceeded to Hartlepool, taking the life-boat with them, and leaving the cobble and six men in extreme peril to get back to Whitby as well they could.*

Meanwhile, the National life-boat No.2, Harriet Forteath, *was got out, and the pilots and fishermen put on their cork jackets, intending to launch her for the benefit of the cobble and her crew, but the Secretary told them that the boat was not got out for that purpose, but merely to let the public see that there was another life-boat, and saying that the cobble was in no danger, although he went immediately to the chief of the Coast Guard and got him to take the rocket apparatus to the harbour mouth and throw a line across, so that if the cobble was swamped the men might get hold of it and so*

*save themselves. Now, the boat would have been launched and put
back again clear of expense to the Institution. The cobble succeeded in
entering the harbour in safety, but if such is to be the practice when
men incur risk to render assistance in cases of distress, we shall on all
occasions have to launch the* Fishermen's Friend, *a private lifeboat, and work against the National life-boats whenever the
opportunity serves us, as the using of the National boats in opposition
to private enterprise is contrary to the Institution's regulations, and is
in effect taking away the bread from our families.*[7]

The letter was signed by John Douglas, Pilot; Samuel Hutchinson,
fisherman; Henry Freeman, fisherman and coxswain of the Upgang
Life-boat; William Cooper; Ralph Storr; and William Austin,
fishermen.

In retaliation, the Local Committee of the RNLI, in collaboration
with the National Office, issued the following letter in defence of the
crew of the *Robert Whitworth*, and in particular, the actions of the
coxswain, Samuel Lacy.

THE NATIONAL LIFEBOATS AND THE COBBLEMEN
Whitby, 2nd November 1875.

*Sir,- As the committee of the Whitby and Upgang Branch of the Royal
National Lifeboat Institution consider the letter published in your last
week's issue is calculated to give the public the wrong impression of the
services rendered by their boat,* Robert Whitworth, *on the 22nd
October, in saving the barque,* Svadsfare *and her crew of sixteen
hands, I beg to hand you a copy of the resolution passed by this
Committee at their meeting held on the first Inst., at which Captain
Ward, RN, Chief Inspector of Lifeboats to the Institution, was present
- viz. that the Committee and Captain Ward not only exonerate
Samuel Lacy, the coxswain, from all blame, but consider he would
have been neglect in his duty had he not proceeded to the assistance of
the barque on perceiving she had shown a signal for aid; and they are
further of the opinion that his doing so did not infringe the rule of the
Institution which requires its boats not to be used so as to interfere with
private enterprise. The subsequent rejection of the services of the cobble
and her crew rested entirely with the captain of the barque, who
naturally preferred that assistance of the safer boat and the larger body
of men to accompany him to Hartlepool.*

*The Committee consider their Hon. Secretary, with the assistance of
Mr Richard Smith, the Chief Officer of Coast Guard, took every
precaution for the safety of the crew of the cobble, and that the*

launching of the No.2 lifeboat was uncalled for. Such, Mr Editor, being the opinion of Captain Ward and a committee of thirteen practical and most of them nautical men, I shall be obliged by your giving this letter publicity in your paper, that the public who support our boats may divest their minds of any wrong impression which they may have formed from the letter you inserted last week. - I remain yours truly, George W Smales, Hon. Secretary.[8]

Notwithstanding this slight blemish on the record of the *Robert Whitworth*, the May of 1876 saw the lifeboat again undertake a joint rescue with the No.2 lifeboat and other rescue services to save a number of fishing cobbles in distress. From the subsequent report in the *Whitby Gazette* it would appear that all bitterness and signs of petty jealous had abated by this time, and it was noted by this date, Henry Freeman had taken over from Samuel Lacy as coxswain of the *Robert Whitworth*.[9]

In the three years between 1877 and the beginning of 1880 the *Robert Whitworth* continued in her valiant service and effected a number of rescues. In total during that period she went to the aid of seven vessels and saved the lives of fifty-five crew and one dog!

On the two days of the 27 and 28 October 1880, the worst storms for many years swept across the British Isles. Reports of damage to property and of extensive flooding came from all parts of the country. In northern England very heavy rain fell continuously for forty-eight hours, and at the same time the gale reached hurricane force. Ships were driven ashore all along the north-east coast; many of them were broken up and their crews washed overboard by tremendous seas before anything could be done to save them. At Whitby, houses were blown down, and the flooded river Esk swept ships from their moorings and took them out to sea or deposited them along the harbourside - but there was no work for the lifeboats until the second day.

Early in the afternoon a schooner was seen in the distance. Her sails had been blown to rags, and she seemed at the mercy of the gale. By good fortune she cleared Whitby Rock, but was

Figure 4. A nineteenth century engraved portrait of Henry Freeman, coxswain of the *Robert Whitworth*, showing him wearing the new cork life-jacket which saved his life in 1861, when he was the sole survivor of a terrible disaster which killed twelve of the lifeboat crew while on a rescue mission - it was, coincidentally, his first day as a lifeboatman! Reproduced from a nineteenth century copy of *Illustrated London News*.

hurled on to the beach. The seas made a complete breach over her; the crew were in imminent danger of being washed overboard. Henry Freeman, coxswain (Figure 4), took out the *Robert Whitworth*, approaching the wreck from seaward with his boat steadied by means of a drogue. Three of the crew of five had been taken into the lifeboat when the drogue-line broke, and the lifeboat was carried to the beach. Two men were still on board the vessel, which was by this time known to be the *Reaper*, of Douglas, Isle of Man.

The Coastguard working from the West Pier, succeeded in putting a line across her and rigged the breeches buoy. The captain of the *Reaper* tried to get into it, but fell into the sea. One of the lifeboat-men, Harrison Hodgson, made an heroic attempt to save him by swimming off from the beach, but was driven back three times. Ropes were thrown, one of which he captain seized, but eventually a tremendous sea appeared to stun him, and he disappeared when he was only fifty yards from the pier. By this time the lifeboat was again alongside the *Reaper*, and took off the remaining man.

A few minutes later a large fishing yawl, the *Good Intent*, of Staithes, struck the each a little north of the *Reaper*. Freeman went out again, and brought in the crew of eight. The yawl was quickly followed by the schooner, *Elizabeth Austen*, which ran ashore opposite the coastguard station. This time, Henry Freeman took the lifeboat *Harriott Forteath*; possibly his own lifeboat *Robert Whitworth* was not yet on her launching carriage, for the three vessels had been flung on shore in rapid succession - notwithstanding, there was no need for haste; the schooner *Elizabeth Austen* was repeatedly buried under enormous seas, and was beginning to break up, but the lifeboat was brought alongside and took off her crew of five, all completely exhausted. A few moments later, the *Elizabeth Austen* was a complete wreck.[10]

Between four and five o'clock that same day, a brigantine was observed on her beam-ends, smothered by great seas. For a time she disappeared, and it was thought the vessel had floundered, but she righted herself and came towards the beach. Her sails had been blown away; she was completely helpless and at the mercy of the furious gale. The ship struck just beyond the West Cliff Saloon and was immediately pounded by very heavy seas. She proved to be the John Snell, of Yarmouth, bound for Newcastle with wheat. Freeman took out the *Robert Whitworth* this time, but had not gone far before the lifeboat was almost overturned, and was carried towards the beach. By valiant efforts, her crew got the *Robert Whitworth* back on course, and after some twenty minutes they reached the *John Snell*.

The ship's crew were completely exhausted, and some of them were injured also. With tremendous difficulty and at great risk they were taken off the wreck and brought ashore.

The courage and endurance of the lifeboat-men that day, 28 October 1880, earned them high praise and the admiration of many. Henry Freeman, coxswain of the *Robert Whitworth,* was awarded a silver clasp to the silver medal he had won on the day he had been the sole survivor of the 1861 lifeboat diaster, when in similar conditions, the lifeboat crew of twelve had perished.[11]

If the rescues of October 1880 were the high-light in an exemplary and distinguished service probably the greatest ignominy in the career of the *Robert Whitworth* was the loss of the brigantine *Lumley* with all hands - certainly, at the least it was the most controversial of all her launchings and rescues, and the results of which were to tax the crew's forbearance to the limit in the wake of the resultant criticism.

> *During the hours of Saturday night an Sunday morning* [16 and 17 January 1881] *the coast immediately lying north of Whitby piers was the scene of a terrible catastrophe. It is unexampled in the history of the shipping disasters on this part of the coast, and it stands out as a solitary instance were the whole available life-saving institutions, - the Royal Naval Brigade, two lifeboats, together with all the supplementary aide which are happily ever present on such occasions, proved of no avail.*
>
> *The night of Saturday was not distinguished in the way of rough weather in a manner which created any apprehensions of any forthcoming disaster on the coast. Certainly there were intermittent snow-storms, and a heavy ground swell falling on the beach, but there was little or no wind except that which blew in a direction which was the least likely to incline any vessel to come too near the shore. Consequently, at a little before ten o'clock, when lights where witnessed from the coastguard station apparently from a ship standing out to the north of Upgang, the idea of any vessel being in danger was received - if received at all in the first instance - with incredulity. The signals, however, was repeated, and as soon as it was understood that assistance was required, so soon were the usual signals given at the coastguard battery, summoning the crews of the local lifeboats and the members of the Royal Naval Life Saving Brigade, and all others whom the serious nature of the circumstances*

Figure 5. The brigantine *Lumley,* of South Shields, in full sail. This was later wrecked off Whitby in January 1861 with the loss of all hands.

might concern.

It was not long before the rocket apparatus was got in readiness, and as soon as it was possible rockets were sent from the beach in the direction of the ship. The larger of the two lifeboats at Whitby belonging to the National Lifeboat Institution - the Robert Whitworth - *under the direction of Mr Henry Freeman, coxswain, was launched down the slipway adjoining the Coastguard Station.*

The lifeboat Joseph Sykes, *at Upgang, also belonging to the Royal National Lifeboat Institution, and under the command of Mr Thomas Langlands as coxswain, was launched at the station.*

The vessel was fixed on the rocks nearly a mile from the foot of Upgang.

The night was very dark, owing to the dense clouds which hung overhead threatening a snowstorm, and nothing could be seen out in the darkness save the glare occasioned by the burning of a tar-barrel on the deck of the stranded ship. For this beacon the [Upgang] *lifeboat steered.*

The place at which the Upgang lifeboat was launched was a rather awkward one, and from the first moment it was seen that it would be impossible to reach the vessel without contending against terrific odds. No sooner had the boat got under way than she was struck by a heavy sea: a sea so ponderous, so unexpected, that it startled the crew, and for a moment seemed to overwhelm the gallant boat.

She, however, soon rallied, her buoyancy and seaworthiness soon exhibiting themselves, and the crew, encouraged by their coxswain [Thos. Langlands], *renewed their efforts and launched out again into the rolling seas.*

The darkness of the night prohibited those on shore witnessing what occurred to the lifeboat, but we have it on testimony which is indisputable that the boat was tossed back by the mighty seas, that the crew renewed their exertions, that again and again they were hurled back, that, after nearly two hours' continuous exertions in the midst of angry seas, during a pitiless snowstorm, the crew struggled bravely, and that, after all, they were unable to get near enough to the vessel to render the least assistance to the crew, whose lives depended, seemingly, altogether upon the help from the shore. . .

During the early period of the night those in charge of the rocket apparatus fired a number of rockets in the direction of the ship, but the best of them fell a long way short. Mr Richard Smith, the chief officer of the Coastguard, did all that was possible under the circumstances, but his experience son led him to understand tat it was not possible to make any of the rockets reach the vessel, so as to establish any communication with the shore. . .

While all this was being enacted at Upgang, the Whitby lifeboat Robert Whitworth *was steadily pursuing her long, wearisome and dangerous course towards the stranded vessel, whose position was indicated by the flare from the burning tar-barrel. The distance from Whitby to where the vessel was laid was about two miles, and through the darkness of the night and through the an angry sea the boat plodded its way. It was an expedition fraught with danger, and one, even under much more favourable circumstances, calculated to test the endurance and zeal of any crew.*

At length the lifeboat came within a quarter of an hour's row of the vessel. The crew then perceived lights on the shore, some of which were moving inland. The coxswain (Mr Freeman) says he saw - or thinks he saw - a blue or green light on the beach, which was taken by him and his crew as an intimation that the crew of the vessel had already been landed safely by the Upgang lifeboat, which they (the Whitby lifeboat crew) knew had put off. Seeing that the light on board the vessel had been extinguished, the original supposition that the crew had been rescued seemed to be confirmed. It seemed useless to go to the ship, and the lifeboat was thereupon turned round, and a light was sown indicating that such and operation had taken place.

A watch was kept on the shore, but no intimation was given for the [Whitby] *lifeboat to stick to the ship.*

As the result proved, a great mistake was made and how it may be cleared up remains to be seen.'

The boat in returning was overtaken by a fearful snowstorm - so dense, indeed, as to obscure from vision all objects usually considered essential to the safe guidance of any craft through the sea. The lifeboat grounded on the sands a little to the north of the foot of the West Cliff Saloon. The crew were much fatigued by their long and arduous row, and by the intense cold which prevailed.

On landing, several of them, under the natural impression that their services would be no longer required on that occasion, went to their homes, while others went on by way of the beach to Upgang. When the crew had separated, news came to hand that the Upgang lifeboat had not, after all, succeeded in her attempt, and Mr Gibson, the harbour master, and local secretary to the Royal National Lifeboat Institution directed that the Robert Whitworth *should be again launched and taken out to the ship, which was yet standing. The coxswain of the boat readily consented, and did his utmost to rally his crew, while there were plenty of volunteers about who were ready to give assistance.*

Unfortunately some delay took place - a delay which no human foresight could have avoided under the singularly exceptional circumstances - and before the lifeboat could be got on to her carriage it was found impossible to convey her by the beach, as the tide had already flowed too high to enable her to be dragged past the point at the Volunteer Battery. Consequently, it was determined - there being yet hope of doing some service - to convey the lifeboat on the high road by Khyber Pass, Skinner-street, St Hilda's-terrace, and so on by Upgang-lane. But before she could be got there the climax had arrived.

The vessel, with all her sails set, had stood out in the blackness of the night, solitary and helpless, with her crew, doubtless half-frozen and trembling for their lives - stood out there for four mortal hours. All about the vessel were dark and angry waters, which for some time could be seen by the lurid, phantom-like glare from the burning tar-barrel, leaping along her side and over her decks. The light had died out gradually, and for a long time nothing could be seen, and not a sound heard beyond the roaring of the waters. At length the moon broke partly through a dense mass of clouds, just sufficiently so to enable those on an elevated position to see the vessel gradually bend before the force of the sea. Slowly she went, almost imperceptibly at first, until she fell or rather laid, on her side, and then it was known that all was over. This was at five minutes past two o'clock on the Sabbath morn, and it was at that time, most likely, when every mortal soul on board passed beyond the limits of all earthly help, into a haven where storms and tempests are unknown.

Before the vessel parted, it was known that her name was the Lumley, *as her name board had already washed ashore, together with a quantity of boards and other wreckage. Subsequent information showed that the vessel was the brig* Lumley, *of South Shields. She was a vessel of 285 tons register, and was commanded by Mr John Woodhouse, an experienced sailor and part owner of the ship. The principal owner was Mr George W Waugh, of South Shields.*

Early on the same morning of the sad catastrophe the body of the captain of the vessel, John Woodhouse, was found on the slipway of the Coastguard Station. The body was laid upwards, with the face embedded in the sand. It was quite rigid - seemingly frozen. It was at once conveyed to a house adjoining the Coastguard. On the following morning the body of A Janson, a fine young fellow of twenty-one, a native of Sweden, was found among the rocks in the Volunteer Battery. . .[12]

Immediately after the incident of the Lumley, Captain Gibson wrote his report for the RNLI, confining his statement to those facts of which he himself had been witness. The result was that he said very little of Henry Freeman's share in the attempt to rescue the crew of the *Lumley*. Gibson had been present when the Upgang lifeboat was launched, and had remained on the beach until she returned two hours later damaged and unsuccessful. Knowing the state of the sea, he could understand why the attempts at rescue had failed. He was able to describe the experience of Langland's crew in some detail; from the exhaustion of the men Gibson realised what a grim ordeal they had endured. In his report he praised their courage and perseverance and made it clear that they had done their utmost to save the lives of the men on the wrecked vessel.

Gibson had seen nothing of Freeman's attempts to reach the *Lumley* from Whitby, indeed, Freeman appears to have launched the *Robert Whitworth* on his own initiative. Consequently, in his report, Gibson merely states that when he reached Whitby he found the *Robert Whitworth* on the beach, near the West Cliff Saloon, having already been afloat. He commended Freeman for his willingness to take the boat by road to Upgang, and concluded his report by repeating that, 'the Whitby boat had already been afloat but had been unable to reach the wreck'. By dismissing Freeman's efforts in this way, Gibson had failed to do justice to a crew which had attempted to perform an exceptionally arduous service in appalling conditions, but he avoided expressing any opinion about the reasons for the failure.

On the Monday morning, the *Yorkshire Post* and the *Northern Echo* printed almost identical accounts of the disaster. Langland and his crew were warmly praised, and their experiences reported in detail. Less space was given to the work of the Whitby crew, though the dangers and hardships they had endured were described in full. The lights seen at Upgang, which caused Henry Freeman to abandon his attempts were mentioned without comment. The Scarborough newspapers published a similar account. At the end of the week, the local paper, the *Whitby Gazette* printed a long account of the occurrence (reproduced above). Once more, Langland's crew were highly praised. In this account, however, Freeman's men were given the credit they deserved for their very gallant work, and their ordeal was more fully described than in any of the other reports. Nevertheless, the writer referred to 'the lights which Mr Freeman saw, or thinks he saw' with a certain amount of scepticism, and suggested that 'a mistake was made or a misapprehension occurred, and how it may be cleared up remains to be seen'.

The affair was in this highly unsatisfactory state when the

Northern Echo published a letter from Sandsend, a tiny fishing hamlet not far from Upgang, written under the pseudonym of 'An Eyewitness'. What prompted this unprovoked attack remains as much a mystery as the actual cause of the *Lumley's* sinking!

LIFEBOAT SERVICES AT WHITBY
To the Editor of the 'Northern Echo'

Sandsend, January 20th, 1881

GENTLEMEN,- I venture to invite the attention of your readers to some facts in connection with the wreck of the brig Lumley *at Whitby, reported in the* Northern Echo *of the 17th Inst. Shortly before ten o'clock on the evening of Saturday, the 16th Inst, signals of distress were observed at Sandsend from a vessel in the direction of Upgang. The readiness with which the Coastguard at Sandsend, with the volunteers of the rocket apparatus, proceeded to the scene of the wreck is very commendable. The impossibility of reaching with the rocket a vessel nearly 700 yards beyond low-water mark soon became evident, and so the Upgang lifeboat, close at hand, was launched after a considerable delay. Subsequent events, however, have shown that it would have been well for the crew of the ill-fated vessel if this delay had been indefinitely protracted.*

It was half past eleven o'clock before the lifeboat, manned with what has been described by one paper, as a rather mixed crew, put out into what has been caused to appear as a terrible sea. The night, however, as the hundreds assembled on the shore can testify, was bright and calm from ten o'clock to nearly an hour past midnight. There was, as usual, a little broken water along the shore, but as the lifeboat is said to have approached within 150 yards of the vessel, this, the faintest approach to "seething waves" must have been passed over safely.

If the observation of old and experienced mariners is of no account, how does the fact that a tar-barrel, around which some of the crew were seen, was blazing for two and a half hours reconcile itself with what has been dramatically described as a "merciless surging sea". If, as was the fact, there was no wind, how is it that a strong wind is said to have detained the Whitby lifeboat for two hours in the space of little more than a mile?

About half-past twelve o'clock a green light, signifying a successful rescue, was shown by one or other of the two lifeboats, and the public, for whose dispersion homeward it was also the signal, did not receive - and then with sorrow not unmingled with indignation -the almost incredible news of the loss of the Lumley's *crew until the morning was*

far advanced. Messengers were despatched again for the Whitby lifeboat - a fact which is suggestive of the opinion of the public concerning the gallantry of a portion at least of the Upgang crew; but the vessel had broken up by three o'clock on Sunday morning, and not one of her men has been left to tell the table of the skilful and fearless efforts made to rescue them.- Yours sincerely,'
AN EYE-WITNESS[13]

It is impossible to reconcile the statements made in this letter with the accounts given by Captain Gibson, and by the newspaper correspondents who all agree that the sea was exceptionally high. All of them speak of the huge waves which nearly swamped the lifeboats. They all refer to the appalling conditions which the men had to face. Only the writer of the letter suggested that there was any delay in launching the Upgang lifeboat; and no else stated that a green light - the signal for 'Rescue completed' - had been shown by a lifeboat.

Not unnaturally, the lifeboat-men were infuriated by the letter. Within two days the RNLI sent down a Captain Nepean, the Royal Navy Inspector of Boats, to hold an enquiry into the whole affair. Captain Gibson, the two coxswains and the Chief Officer of the Coastguard also gave evidence. It was established that the *Lumley* had been end on to the sea, affording no lee for the lifeboat to approach her; that the boats had been promptly launched and well-manned, and that the crews had endured two hours of exhaustive labour in a very rough sea.

The real point of issue, however, was the green or blue light which Freeman had taken to be a signal from shore to show that the rescue had ben completed. His credit as a coxswain depended on being able to establish that he had been justified in turning back when only a quarter of an hour's pulling from the wreck. The Committee agreed that 'a light on shore, viewed from seaward in the glamour of a snow storm would appear blue'. This opinion, accepted as it was by a Committee which was largely made up of experienced sea-captains, fully vindicated Freeman's action in abandoning his attempt to reach the *Lumley*. Captain Nepean and the Committee thanked both crews for their efforts and expressed their complete confidence in all concerned. The Chief Officer of Coastguards said that in his opinion no lifeboat could have saved the men of the Lumley in such a sea; other members of the Committee commented scathingly on the writer of the letter published by the *Northern Echo*.

It is difficult to see how the Committee could have come to any other conclusion. Their findings appear to have been in accordance with the known facts, and in any case, they could hardly have been too critical with Freeman just at that time, for between the loss of the *Lumley* and the date of the enquiry, he and his men had become national heroes, having done a deed which even today, ranks as one of the finest feats ever performed by a lifeboat crew.

On the very day that the *Lumley* sank at Whitby, despite a hard frost, frequent falls of snow and the heavy seas which had wreaked havoc on the *Lumley*, the brigantine *Visitor* sailed from the Tyne for London, coal-laden. She was an old vessel, about 200 tons, built at Sunderland in 1823, registered at Whitby, and owned at Robin Hood's Bay. She carried a crew of five under her master, Captain Anderson.

After the *Visitor* had set sail, the weather rapidly deteriorated. Inland, there were reports of deaths from exposure so bad was the cold. The whole country was snow-bound. Railway trains were halted by the weather, roads were blocked by enormous drifts. Bristol was cut-off from the rest of England. Off shore, the wind was rising, and the seas, already heavy, were increasing in violence.

Two days later, on the afternoon of Tuesday, 18 January [1881], the *Visitor* had reached Flamborough, having passed by Whitby, suddenly the wind changed direction and rose to a full south-easterly gale. The brig was driven northward before it, back on its previous course. Most of the sails were ripped away, and she began to fill steadily with water. Very early on the morning of Wednesday, her captain realised that he was in danger of being blown ashore on a rocky coast, so he chose to anchor in the comparative shallow water of Robin Hood's Bay hoping to ride out the storm. There was by now two feet of water in the hold. The *Visitor* lay at anchor about two miles south of the township. By eight o'clock the water in the hold had risen to five feet, and waves were breaking right over the deck and it seemed the brigantine would not remain afloat much longer.

Her lifeboat, secured by a kedge and two warps, was put over the side, and five of the crew including Captain Anderson, scrambled into her. The last to leave the *Visitor* was A C Dodd, the apprentice. The others shouted to him to 'be sharp'; but in the noise and confusion he mistook the call for an order to 'cast off'. He did so, but before Dodd could jump to the lifeboat the boat drifted a little way from the brig, though close enough to be sheltered from the full force of the waves. About an hour later, the *Visitor* went down at anchor. As she sank, Dodd in desperation, lashed himself to a lifebuoy, jumped into the seas, and swam to the lifeboat. The five men pulled him in, and there the six remained, waiting for daylight and knowing that only the slight shelter of the wrecked brig prevented then from being driven on the rocks which fringed the bay.

Ashore, nothing was known of the fate of the *Visitor* until her quarter-board was found washed up on the beach later that day, and as the light improved, the coastguards sighted the boat still in the lee of the wreck. Too far out for a rescue by means of rockets and lines; the only way it was realised to reach her was from seawards. The private lifeboat at Robin Hood's Bay was old and had been neglected for many years; the local fishermen declined to launch her, as they regarded the boat as unseaworthy, and the coastguards, having examined the lifeboat, gave instructions that she was not to be used. The correctness of the decision has never been disputed.

Despite bitter winds and the snow showers, men gathered in groups to see what was happening and consider the situation. The vicar, the Reverend J Cooper and his son joined one group which was discussing what could be done for the crew in their precarious position. At length someone suggested that an appeal for help should be sent to Whitby. A sailor would probably have said at once that it was impossible to row a lifeboat from Whitby in such a storm, but the Reverend Cooper, eager to seize any chance sent a telegram worded, 'Vessel sunk, crew in open boat riding by wreck, send Whitby life-boat if practicable.'

The telegram was received at Whitby a little after ten o'clock in the morning. The Lifeboat Committee, coxswain, and crew held a consultation.

A first suggestion was that the lifeboat could be towed round to Robin Hood's Bay, about ten miles by sea, by steam tug; but this was impossible, as no tug could survive such a storm as was then raging. The next suggestion was to man the lifeboat and pull round. This was put to the vote and unanimously rejected. With the ebb tide and the furious gale against them, no boat's crew in the world could have taken the lifeboat to the wreck, even if there had been a hope of living in that tremendous storm. It was then that Captain Gibson, lifeboat secretary, proposed that the lifeboat could be taken overland, a distance of six miles - yet six miles of hill and moor, yet no sooner was the plan spoke then it was adopted, and 'with praiseworthy promptitude' a large number of men with shovels were despatched by Captain Gibson to clear the roads where necessary, 'telegraphing at the same time to Robin Hood's Bay for men to be sent off to cut [through] the snow-drifts, and for horses to meet the lifeboat.'

The *Robert Whitworth* was got out of her house and dragged by hand up the Pier, across the bridge and down Church-street, where

Figure 6. A nineteenthth century engraving depicting the *Robert Whitworth* being hauled overland to Robin Hood's Bay to effect the rescue of the brigantine Visitor. A triumphant success and fitting conclusion to the career of the lifeboat *Robert Whitworth*.

a number of horses were attached to the carriage, and at time as many as eighteen horses were employed. Although the snow lay deep the lifeboat was got along with great success. Fortunately amongst those who obeyed the telegraphic instructions was Mr Matthew Wellburn, who met the [life]boat near Stainsacre, where he was requested by Captain Gibson and coxswain Henry Freeman to take command, and from that moment forward never a hitch occurred. Silence was maintained, snow drifts disappeared or the boat was dragged through them.

In one part of the journey the high road was diverted from, the gateway was widened, and a shorter and less hazardous cut was made through Mrs Attlay's field. The journey was not accomplished without great labour, and it was not until the expiration of nearly three hours that the lifeboat reached Bay Bank top, where the horses were unyoked, and here the scene was of indescribable interest. The immense crowd of people were completely overpowered with the sight of the towering lifeboat and the mass of men who had come on their mission of mercy.

The boat was lowered down with ropes by men, under the command of Mr Wellburn, the shafts being in charge of ten men acquainted with the difficulties of the work, and well they managed, as those who know the intricate road and the turn at Mr Edward Martin's corner can well understand. The men were cheered and encouraged by Mr Gibson and Mr Henry Freeman, and it was creditable to the farmers and others resident near the line of march that they were very ready in volunteering to give all the assistance in their power.

On arrival at Robin Hood's Bay the lifeboat crew were received with marked expressions of welcome . . . As soon as possible the lifeboat was launched. There was a heavy sea but notwithstanding the difficulties which the Whitby crew had gone through they rowed out in the thick of it, and were much cheered. They had great odds to contend with. Several times they were nearly swamped, and one sea fell upon them with such force so as to break no less than six oars, and so disable the boat. The crew had already been out for nearly an hour, rowing at full strength. They were by this time partly exhausted, and the coxswain, Mr Henry Freeman, finding it impossible to make headway under such circumstances, turned the boat and proceeded again for shore. Two of the crew had to be taken from the boat, and the coxswain called for reinforcement. Several Whitby men at once came forward, but only one Bay man (John Skelton) was taken on board.

The lifeboat, being [now] partly double-banked, proceeded out to sea again; they had a hard struggle, but after about three quarters of an hour's row succeeded in reaching the boat that contained the crew of the sunken vessel. The poor fellows were in a half frozen state, having been out in the sea for about seven hours exposed to the frost and the snow, and in imminent peril of their lives from the seas which fell upon them.

Figure 7. A photograph of the crew of the lifeboat *Robert Whitworth* taken in the nineteenth century shortly after the rescue of the brigantine *Visitor*, with coxswain Henry Freeman in the centre. *Loaned by Mrs Annie Parker.*

On the [life]boat nearing the shore the hundreds who had assembled and witnessed the bravery and endurance of the Whitby men set up a cheer. On being landed the crew of the foundered vessel were in the last stages of exhaustion, most of them speechless, and it is believed that had they been exposed for an hour or two longer they would have died of starvation. Certainly, if the Whitby lifeboat had been taken on to Robin Hood's Bay in the manner she was - if the Whitby lifeboat-men had not acted with the gallantry they did - these six poor fellows, who formed the crew of the *Visitor*, of Whitby, would have perished.

Whilst the boat was away the most intense anxiety was felt in Whitby as to the progress of her mission, and information was supplied by telegraph as to her movements, and duly posted in the *Gazette*[14] office window, in Bridge-street, and great was the relief and the manifestations of joy which ran through the town when it was known that perfect success had crowned the Herculean labours of the men, and that a crew of six hands were saved from inevitable death.'[15]

The *Robert Whitworth* was left at Robin Hood's Bay until the storm subsided some days later, then her crew walked from Whitby to row her back to the lifeboat station.

In the enthusiasm aroused by the rescue of the crew of the *Visitor*, the recriminations caused by the failures at Upgang the previous week were forgotten. The courage and endurance of the lifeboatmen were extolled in the national press, the Royal National Lifeboat Institution officially thanked them for their services, both to the *Lumley* and to the *Visitor*, and paid them double the normal rates for both launches. Locally, they were entertained to dinner, a subscription was raised for their benefit, and they were invited to attend a public thanksgiving at St Michael's church. There was a general feeling of goodwill towards the men. Adults spontaneously made gifts to coxswain Henry Freeman for distribution among the crew, and two little children gave 7d 'to help replace the oars broken at Robin Hood's Bay.'

Following that momentous day, the *Robert Whitworth* saw no more rescues in her capacity as No.1 lifeboat at Whitby. While at sea on exercise on the 4 March 1881, second coxswain James Pounder collapsed and died. Later in the year, the *Robert Whitworth* was replaced, ten years of stalwart service came to an end when a new lifeboat was allocated to Whitby No.1 station in December 1881.

As to the final fate of the *Robert Whitworth*, RNLI and local records appear uncertain as to her end. The *Robert Whitworth* was not recorded as being transferred to service at either the Whitby No.2 station, nor the Upgang lifeboat-house - yet one authority states that on the 8 October 1892 - a further ten years on from her 'official' retirement - she was launched to the rescue of the local cobble *Palm Branch* with a crew of three, which was being driven toward the notorious Whitby Rock. The time was 3.30pm. It was high tide and, as heavy seas were breaking right up the slipway down to the beach, the *Robert Whitworth* was lowered into the harbour using the crane at Scotch Head. Henry Freeman was still at the helm as coxswain, and he and his crew battled their way out through atrocious waves watched by a large crowd, and after an hour, they successfully succeeded in saving all hands[16] – a fitting climax to a noble career, and bringing the total number of lives saved by the *Robert Whitworth* to 128 – the highest total recorded in the history of any Whitby rowing lifeboat.

Service Record of the Whitby Lifeboat *Robert Whitworth*

1870 July 26[17]   Brigantine, *Mary & Jane*, of Sunderland; assisted to save vessel and four crew.

1871 October 2   Schooner, *Dispatch*, of Whitby; saved three crew.

October 3   Schooner, *Dispatch*; reboarded crew.

December 6   Four fishing cobbles, of Whitby; saved twelve crew.

1875 October 18   Barque, *Teazer*, of Whitby; saved nine crew.

October 20   Barque, *Godstadt Minde*, of Tonsberg; abandoned, no crew, left to drift (came ashore north of Staithes).

October 22   Barque, *Svadsfare*, of Porsgrund, Norway; saved sixteen crew and vessel.

1876 May 24   One fishing cobble, of Whitby; saved three crew.

1877 February 23   Fishing cobble, *Anne Elizabeth*, of Whitby; landed three crew (one dead).

March 1   Boat of brigantine, *Christopher Hansteen*, of Christiana, Norway; saved eight crew and one dog.

1878 January 5   Steamship, *Oscar*, of Leith; saved twenty-two crew.

January 6   Steamship, *Oscar*; reboarded captain to save papers and instruments.

May 8	Fishing cobbles, *Eliza* and *James & Sarah*, of Scarborough; saved vessel and four crew.
September 12	Number of fishing cobbles off Whitby, boarded crews and stood by. Fishing cobble, *Welcome*, of Hartlepool; saved two crew.
1879 March 12	Steamship, *Lorentzen*, of London; saved seventeen crew.
1880 October 28	Schooner, *Reaper*, of Douglas (IoM); saved four crew.
October 28	Fishing yawl, *Good Intent*, of Staithes; saved eight crew.
October 28	Schooner, *John Snell*, of Great Yarmouth; saved five crew.
1881 January 16	Brigantine, *Lumley*, of South Shields; all hands lost.
January 19	Brigantine, *Visitor*; saved six crew.
1892 October 8[18]	Fishing cobble, *Palm Branch*, of Whitby; saved three crew.

Notes and References

1. *Lifeboat*, Vol.VIII, No.87, p397
2. *ibid*. Vol.VII, No.86, p239
3. *ibid*. Vol.VIII, No.87, p.397
4. *Whitby Gazette*, Saturday, 23 October 1875
5. *ibid.*
6. *ibid*. Saturday, 30 October 1875
7. *Whitby Times*, 29 October 1875
8. *ibid*. 5 November 1875
9. *Whitby Gazette*, 27 May 1876
10. The remains of the vessel *Elizabeth Austen* lay buried in sand until March 1883, when another terrific storm uncovered the wreckage and washed it further up on to the beach.
11. Humble, A F *The Rowing Lifeboats of Whitby*.
12. *Whitby Gazette*, 21 January 1881
13. *Northern Echo*, January 1881
14. Whitby Gazette offices
15. *Whitby Gazette*, January 1881
16. Morris, Jeff *The Story of the Whitby Lifeboats*
17. Lifeboat as yet without a name, but locally called the *Lucy*.
18. Launched in the capacity of reserve boat. See, Morris, Jeff *The Story of the Whitby Lifeboats*.

CONTRIBUTORS

1. HEARTS OF OAK – WHITBY WHALERS

Kate Bonella was born in Nottingham in 1953. She has spent most of her

life in Yorkshire, Cleveland and Northumbria doing a variety of jobs ranging from selling *Encyclopedia Britannica* to teaching art and craft as a nursing assistant in a Medium Secure Unit for men with learning disabilities. In 1997 Kate returned to full-time education and lived in Oxford for a year whilst studying history and historiography for a Certificate in Higher Education at Ruskin College. Her article on whaling is a much reduced version of a third term project there. She is now a mature student at St Andrew's university reading medieval history and archaeology. Kate has a son, of whom she is excessively proud, and a grandson.

2. JOHN PAUL JONES – THE TURNCOAT HERO

Jack Storer is a retired sugar-boiler, who after the war, worked for many

famous sweet manufacturers throughout England. Later, he produced sticks of rock for the seaside industry, and was one of the first to introduce the 'Three Legs' design into rock on the Isle of Man, where he lived for a period. A one-time property owner and shop proprietor, he now lives in Doncaster with his wife Hilda and their pedigree Minature Yorkshire Terrier, Rosie. Jack lists his hobbies as gardening, playing snooker and having a 'quiet tipple' down at the Old Comrades Club.

3. NOW SHOWING – THE CINEMAS OF BRIDLINGTON

David Wright was born in Bridlington in 1945. After a basic education he left school in 1960 and followed various professions in his hometown until 1963, then spent four years in West London. Returning to Bridlington in 1967 he obtained a post with the then Yorkshire Electricty Board (YEB) with which he was employed for the following twenty-five years. Married in 1970, he and his wife Carole have three grown-up children. Work published over four decades includes record and book reviews, short stories, poetry, local interest articles and other offerings featured in publications as diverse as *Ludd's Mill* and *Pennine Platform*. He has had seven collections of verse published over the years; the last of which was by Grafitti Petals Publications, of Houston, Texas. David has also completed an extensive family history in 1997, and is currently working on a series of local interest essays entitled, *Riding East - Tales from the Coast and Wolds*.

4. WISH YOU WERE HERE! THE HOLIDAY JOURNAL OF
GEORGE EATON OF NORWICH
7. SHIP CARVINGS IN WHITBY PARISH CHURCH

Andrew White has spent over a quarter of a century working in museums and archaeology. He studied for an MA in Classics at Lancaster University and for a Ph.D in Archaeology at Nottingham University. A Fellow of the Museums Association and of the Society of Antiquaries, he is married with three children, and is presently Curator of Lancaster City Museums. In his spare time he writes, lectures and broadcasts on local history subjects. Dr White's ancestors have lived in Whitby for more than two hundred years, mostly as mariners, which probably accounts for his lifelong affection for the town and his fascination with its history.

5. Early Aviators of the East Coast
11. The Story of the Whitby Lifeboat Robert Whitworth

Alan Whitworth trained at Bradford College of Art, but from 1977, after a number of years in the world of printing and graphic art, he predominately turned his attention to promoting the preservation of English parish churches, founding and running a charity to that end, writing and lecturing on the subject, mounting many exhibitions promoting the beauty of our homeland churches and organising the first national conference dealing with churches and tourism; and yet his interests are wider, and his regard for old buildings and history has led in one area to the founding of the Yorkshire Dovecote Society after a study of dovecotes and pigeon-lofts, about which he has written and lectured often, and in another, to compile a number of visual records about places with which he has been associated. He now writes and lectures about local history subjects and his books include *Exploring Churches* (in association 1986, 1993); *Yorkshire Windmills* (1991); *Village Tales - The Story of Scalby* (1993); *A History of Bradley* (1998) and *A Travellers Guide to the Esk Valley Railway* (1998).

6. The Corn Windmills of Scarborough & District

Edna Whelan hails from the Bronte country, and while living in Skipton, served as a town councillor. She adores the wind-swept moors and heather, but her greatest delight is the open sea. She has an in-born love of adventure and has had - and in her seventies, is still having a varied life with many interests, painting, caving, studying ancient and medieval history, to name but a few. She is also an authority on Holy Wells about which she has written often, and is a member of the Holy Wells Research and Preservation Group. Edna now lives in Whitby where she met and joined in the adventures of Captain Jack Lammiman, which she shared in her book, The *Helga Maria* (Caedmon Publishers, 1992) which later formed the basis for a film about the life and voyages of Jack Lammiman starring Bob Hoskins. A widow, she keeps in touch with her sons and daughter and five grandchildre

8. HAPPY DAYS – IMAGES OF EDWARDIAN FILEY

Michael Fearon was born in Filey in the late-1920s, and his home has always been there. After school in Bridlington, army service in the Far East and a course of study at the University of Leeds, he lectured in Physics at Hull Nautical College and Humberside College of Higher Education. He has been closely involved with the Filey Museum since its inception in 1970 and is currently its Honorary Assistant Curator. A member of Filey Town Council from 1982 to 1991, Michael Fearon served as Mayor of Filey from 1988 to 1990. He is also the author of a book on Filey history entitled, *Filey; From Fishing Villahe to Spa Resort.*

9. DOVECOTES AND PIGEON LOFTS OF THE EAST COAST

Reg Brunton is married to Sarah and they live in Teeside and have one daughter, Victoria, who is now at university. An employee of ICI Wilton, he has an interest in computers and a fascination with dovecotes. A member of the Yorkshire Dovecote Society, in his youth Reg, named after his father, lived at Whitby, where his mother still resides, and has for a time lived and worked in Africa.

10. ANNIE'S TALE – MEMORIES OF LIFE IN WHITBY

Annie Parker, nee Hansell, was born in March 1921 at No.6 Henrietta Street, Whitby. She went to Cholmley Infant School as a young child and later attended St Michael's school (now demolished). Leaving school at fourteen years of age, Annie first workd at her Granny Wood's fish shop, but moved later to Woolworth's departmental store. When war broke out she was directed to work on munitions in Birmingham, but in 1942 she married Ken Parker, from Whitby, who was then serving in the RAF and returned to Whitby. He had paid court to Annie since she was fourteen. They had four children, two sons, Derek an David and two daughters, Doreen and Jean. Her husband Ken on leaving the RAF after the war, became a marine engineer to the fishing fleet and was well-known in the town until he died in February 1998. Annie Parker has seven grandchildren and now lives next-door to her daughter Jean. Her hobby is gardening.

INDEX OF PLACES

Index of People